From
SILOS
to
SYSTEMS

To our educating colleagues,
who shared their wisdom and animated our work.

From
SILOS
to
SYSTEMS

Reframing
Schools
for
Success

Sally B. Kilgore // Karen J. Reynolds

CORWIN
A SAGE Company

Cover photo by Chris Stein (Getty Images)

For information:

Corwin	SAGE India Pvt. Ltd.
A SAGE Company	B 1/I 1 Mohan Cooperative
2455 Teller Road	Industrial Area
Thousand Oaks, California 91320	Mathura Road,
(800) 233-9936	New Delhi 110 044
Fax: (800) 417-2466	India
www.corwin.com	
SAGE Ltd.	SAGE Asia-Pacific Pte. Ltd.
1 Oliver's Yard	33 Pekin Street #02-01
55 City Road	Far East Square
London EC1Y 1SP	Singapore 048763
United Kingdom	

Printed in the United States of America.

Library of Congress Cataloging-in-Publication Data

Kilgore, Sally.
From silos to systems : reframing schools for success / Sally B. Kilgore, Karen J. Reynolds.
 p. cm.
Includes bibliographical references and index.
ISBN 978-1-4129-7308-3 (pbk. : alk. paper)
 1. School management and organization—United States. 2. Educational leadership—United States. 3. School improvement programs—United States. 4. Organizational effectiveness. I. Reynolds, Karen J. II. Title.

LB2805.K47 2011
371.200973—dc22   2010026678

This book is printed on acid-free paper.

10   11   12   13   14   10   9   8   7   6   5   4   3   2   1

Acquisitions Editor:	Arnis Burvikovs
Associate Editor:	Desirée A. Bartlett
Editorial Assistant:	Kimberly Greenberg
Production Editor:	Cassandra Margaret Seibel
Typesetter:	C&M Digitals (P) Ltd.
Proofreader:	Gretchen Treadwell
Indexer:	Jean Casalegno
Cover Designer:	Anthony Paular and Scott Van Atta
Permissions Editor:	Karen Ehrmann

Contents

List of Figures and Tables

Preface

The fate of this nation rests on many shoulders—but none more heavily than those of our public school educators. It is the talented youth they discover and nourish who will become the entrepreneurs in business and conscientious citizens in our communities.

For educators to carry such a heavy weight, they need an opportunity to reframe how professional life in schools is organized. Schools need, for once, to be a place where other organizations look for guidance in how to make things work—how voices are heard, how innovation occurs, and how lives are transformed.

Many schools are on the cusp of such a transformation. Professional learning communities are bubbling up within and across schools—looking at student work, digging deeper into the underlying concepts of various disciplines, and gaining a better appreciation for how students learn. Some meet weekly in their school, others twitter daily about some immediate concern, and yet others work online with fellow educators in far flung places.

These energetic silos of innovation and reflection will accomplish much but not all that is essential for the needed transformation of our public schools. They cannot surmount the concerned parents who inadvertently make school more difficult for their children or the taunting that some students dole out to the more vulnerable in their midst. Most schools are not organized to help willing, but clueless, staff adopt new technologies or get the data they need to help the students they serve. Educators seldom have the crosscutting ties they need to look at instructional issues in different ways or to see talents in the young that remain invisible in their own classroom.

This book is about the conditions needed to use systems thinking in schools. Applying a systems thinking approach allows organizations to uncover and adopt solutions that avoid unanticipated consequences. For schools, systems thinking provides a strategy for tackling the multiple roadblocks to improving student learning. For instance, high rates of absenteeism in a school may occur not simply because parents are unaware of the fact that their children never get on the bus, but also because some students are bored, others fear the taunting of their peers, and yet others just need to study for a tough exam. For meaningful change to occur, schools need to address all of the roadblocks, not just one of them.

Here we introduce structures and processes that allow teachers to improve student learning and well-being and principals to enable voices to be heard beyond the classroom walls and provide support for innovative classroom practices. It will be most appreciated by administrators whose responsibilities make it difficult to interact daily with teachers. They may confront issues of communication and coordination that limit their ability to provide personal support to each teacher, find innovation languishing for lack of support, or find that expertise never seems to be where one needs it.

Our interest in reorganizing school life in ways that allow educators to work smarter, not harder, began in the early 1990s. We began our journey as part of the New American School's effort to design "world class" models for schools in the 21st century—working to pilot and bring to scale the Modern Red SchoolHouse (MRSH) design. While we both had a passion for building thriving public schools in our nation, one came to the challenge with more bookish knowledge and the other was blessed with more seasoned and practical knowledge of both public schools and business practices. The piloting and bringing to scale of the MRSH design allowed us the opportunity to assess which organizational infrastructure makes a difference for both students and educators.

While our comprehensive design had a number of components, the organizational framework we chose proved to be one of the more significant aspects of our design for 21st-century schools. We introduced a simple structural change in how school administrators garner advice from school staff, coordinate changes in practice, and develop expertise among their educators. While leadership teams were common in the 1990s, teachers' voices remained muted. Yet, all teachers could and should contribute to school life outside their classrooms.

Unleashing the hidden expertise and commitment of teachers created a synergy of great proportions. One Florida teacher, commenting on her experience said: "There is a huge difference in school culture when a staff feels that what they say actually matters. An idea they have could actually come to fruition. The school stops being a place where things happen to you and starts being a place where you can make things happen."

In those modest, but visionary, beginnings, we were fortunate to have colleagues who advised us. Finlay McQuade provided us with a practical as well as scholarly understanding of the challenges in developing transformative instructional programs. Rob Melnick and Lou Ann Bierlain gave us insight into the potential of technology, not simply in terms of instructional resources, but in ways that technology could improve communication and productivity. Susan Barker, who led MRSH's development at the elementary level, helped us see the need to distribute expertise within grade levels or departments. Tim and Paula Gaddis not only took risks as innovators but also ensured a commitment to excellence permeated our work. Genie DePolo and Marci Kozinn's practical experience and persistent questions about most everything (we are smiling) gave us both wisdom and inspiration.

The effort to create this manuscript benefited greatly from our assistants, Chriscynthia Ferrell and Judy Lyles. Their commitment to "doing it right" in terms of details, style, and format made our tasks much easier. We could not have done this without them. For any manuscript prepared by someone in a Kilgore family, nothing is final until Carol Kilgore puts her critical eye over each page. We were beneficiaries of this tradition.

Laci Coppins, Roxie McBride, Suzette Brown Miller, Anne Mitchell, Joyce Pully, and Maryanne Roesch—wise and experienced practitioners all—gave us invaluable feedback as our work progressed. Our husbands, Tom and Bill, were patient cheerleaders. Most important of all, though, are the hundreds of principals and teachers who worked with us—taking risks and providing the evidence that with the right structure and processes, the quality of professional life can become invigorating and greatly increase student learning and well-being.

Acknowledgments

C orwin would like to acknowledge the following peer reviewer for his editorial insight and guidance:

Rob Kesselring, Director
Staff Development Programs
Youth Frontiers Inc.
Minneapolis, MN

About the Authors

Sally B. Kilgore is president and CEO of Modern Red SchoolHouse Institute. Her work has appeared in *Harvard Education Review, Sociology of Education,* and *American Sociological Review.* In the early 1980s, she coauthored *High School Achievement* with Thomas Hoffer and the noted scholar, James S. Coleman. She has served on the editorial boards of the *American Education Research Journal, Sociology of Education,* and *Review of Research in Education.* In the 1980s, she served as the director of the Office of Research (OERI) for the U.S. Department of Education. During the 1990s, she served on the advisory board for the National Center for Education Statistics. She has served on the faculties of Emory University, University of Cincinnati, and Huston-Tillotson College and as an adjunct at Vanderbilt's Peabody School of Education.

She holds a bachelor of arts from Baylor University and a doctorate in sociology from the University of Chicago. She lives in Bell Buckle, Tennessee, with her husband, Tom Cooper.

Karen J. Reynolds has served as an organizational consultant and facilitator to businesses and schools for over 20 years. While working with MRSH, she has coached teams and principals in large inner-city, suburban, and rural districts across the United States. She specializes in helping administrators and school leadership teams design and guide the improvement efforts in their schools. She also works individually with principals as they guide their schools through changes and transitions.

She currently serves as the lead facilitator MRSH's federally funded research initiative Systems Leadership in Middle Schools. Over the course of 20 years, she grew to understand school improvement issues from a variety of perspectives: as a classroom teacher, an administrator at both the elementary and secondary level, and, finally as a central office administrator. Her experience as an upper-level manager of communications and public affairs at the corporate office of a large insurance company gave her the opportunity to understand and work with schools from the community and business world perspective.

She holds a bachelor's degree in education and master's in school administration from Indiana University. She also graduated from the Experiential Preparation for Preparing School Principals (EPPSP Class #1), a two-year postgraduate program, at Butler University. She and her husband, Bill, live in Noblesville, Indiana.

Section I

When it comes to the organizational life in public schools, only American universities do it more ineptly. New problems require new committees. New programs get their own task forces. When programs fizzle, the committee or task force disappears. Principals may want to share leadership, but invariably all the advisory groups, committees, and tasks forces introduce more complexities and responsibilities than solutions. Each department or grade level may have strong collegial relations, but they seldom see the whole picture. Educators with expertise needed to help others adopt new technologies are seldom spread evenly over departments or grades. We propose a structure that endures beyond a single program or individual initiatives and a process for developing expertise and vetting options.

The first section of this book, Chapters 1 through 5, focuses on the organizational processes and structure that schools need. In Chapter 1, we discuss the need to reframe professional life. In Chapter 2, we merge the scholarship of organizational psychologists and sociologists with that of the business researchers to identify the structural characteristics needed to reframe professional life. Basically, who should be at which table?

Reframing professional life to allow for systems thinking requires action teams focused on core dimensions of schooling: curriculum and instruction, technology, school culture and climate, family and community partnerships, professional development, and data analysis. Rather than adding teams and committees to an already cluttered picture, we provide a strategy for consolidating existing groups into teams to address core issues. A guiding coalition links directly with six action teams whose membership includes one or more representatives from each grade level or department. Action teams have the greatest impact when their activities target the same school goal.

Chapter 3 guides teams as they consider the procedures, norms, and expectations needed to be productive in meaningful ways. In brief, how do they do their work?

In Chapter 4, we describe the typical frustrations and challenges that a school confronts when it seeks to make major changes. Frustrations arise with major change simply because one's effectiveness usually diminishes before it improves. Changes in classroom practices, for instance, are accompanied by instances where software instructions were vague, students became confused, or equipment didn't work as promised. How do educators keep such frustrations from derailing the effort? We discuss the conditions that make changes in professional practice worthwhile, how some changes in practice are more drastic and challenging than others, and what researchers find as the requisite steps for successful change.

Chapter 5 focuses on barriers and pitfalls that educators encounter when adopting any change effort, but, in particular, one that involves action teams and collaborative efforts. Barriers to improving practices refer to prior beliefs, norms, and routines shared by the school community that can compromise any effort to improve practice. Pitfalls are common—even predictable— problems that emerge during a change in practices that can lead to lower levels of commitment. It's our dashboard warning system and diagnostic handbook rolled into one.

CHAPTER ONE

Why Reframe Professional Lives of Educators?

O ur interest in reframing the professional lives of educators began some 15 years ago. Working with highly committed and creative teachers as well as dedicated principals who sought to transform their schools, we sensed that the long hours they spent seldom brought the results they wanted. Often, we witnessed frustration and disenchantment. Why couldn't we find a way for educators to overcome the barriers they encounter in realizing the goals they have for the students they serve?

Over the years, we developed a model for designing the professional life of schools that enables educators to work smarter, not more, and achieve the goals they set for themselves and for their students. It is a model based on systems thinking and designed to help educators manage the ever-changing conditions and expectations thrust upon them. The model also helps dissolve the frequent frustrations that arise from great ideas seldom realized, great plans thrown in the circular file, or much effort expended to produce only meager results. Despite the shifts in expectations and needs of educators in the past 20 years, the way we organize professional lives remains largely the same.

Even as late as the 1990s, the daily life of a teacher resembled that of the independent contractor who only shared the school's parking lot with other educators. With the classroom door closed, teachers honed their craft as educational entrepreneurs.

By 2001, public accountability for student performance that attached labels to students and schools became almost universal in the United States. The structure of professional life changed. Fewer independent contractors occupied classrooms—at least in the subjects and grades responsible for creating the accountability labels. Now, educators frequently collaborate within grade- and subject-level teams creating vibrant, but inwardly focused, silos of professionalism. Teachers not involved in the proficiency triathlon—usually kindergarten through second-grade teachers in elementary schools; social studies, art, music, and vocational/ technical teachers at the secondary level; and physical education teachers at all levels—often live "outside" these silos. Yet, many of the problems, as well as the solutions, exist outside the silos.

Certainly, many educators find the 30 years of national concern about public schools a bit tiring. Reform fatigue hits many. Establishing a robust and adaptable system for organizational learning, however, will be essential as schools continue to be subjected to mandates from local, state, and federal entities. Educators enter yet another phase of new expectations—to adopt more rigorous academic standards, intensify their reliance on diagnostic data to determine student needs, and expand their instructional tool kits to address the diverse learning needs of students. With the right structure for processing and absorbing these waves of change, teachers and students can thrive.

Peter Senge (1990) introduced systems thinking to educators. What was (and still is) missing are the structures and processes schools need for systems thinking to make a difference. We seek to provide educators the missing tools to develop what organizational gurus call "the learning organization." Envisioned by Donald Schon (1973), a learning organization is one that is "capable of bringing about its own transformation" (p. 28). You may be working in a learning organization if you don't recall thinking, "Here we go again." But creating that condition requires that we pay attention to how we organize professional life at schools—how information flows, the form in which leadership is shared, the diversity of perspectives we use to solve problems, and the degree to which our interdependence as educators becomes an opportunity rather than a nightmare. We need ways in which teachers are heard and principals gain some relief.

Before we dig deeper into what it means to be a learning organization, we consider cases where things are not working. Scientists usually cannot understand the importance of certain aspects of human systems until things fall apart, that is, when things break down or don't seem to work as expected. For instance, if we all have strong support networks in our lives, we cannot appreciate their value. If we begin by reviewing cases where organizational structures or processes compromise the quality of decisions, we can better appreciate the types of structures and processes that can improve school situations. In this chapter, we gain a better understanding of the importance of certain school practices by reviewing cases where things are not working as they should. In the next chapter, we take on the serious business of understanding what a learning organization relying on systems thinking looks like, and the structure and processes needed to support it.

ORGANIZATIONAL PROBLEMS

Case 1: Constipating Structures

Some years ago, the state of California decided to enhance the leadership skills of its teachers. Principals from all over the state identified teachers from each of their schools for a summer workshop designed to improve strategies for identifying problems and evaluating alternative solutions. Researchers subsequently met with the teachers and principals to assess the impact. For several years, the training had little discernable impact, yet the teachers considered the summer training highly effective (Chrispeels & Martin, 2002). Why this disconnect?

Few of the teachers who attended the workshop became (or were already) members of a school leadership team. Despite this, most met regularly at each of their respective schools. They identified school problems, analyzed possible solutions, and, in some cases, made recommendations to their principal. In one school, newly trained teacher-leaders reviewed the challenges faced by their school and concluded that the class schedule was a great impediment to learning and needed to be changed. With great enthusiasm, they discussed their recommendation with the principal. She promptly dismissed it. A reasonable inference, not mentioned in the case study, concerns future actions of these teachers and their principal: The teachers likely closed their classrooms' doors and avoided professional responsibilities beyond their classrooms. The principal likely acquired further evidence that one should avoid recruiting teacher-leaders for fear that some unworkable proposal emerges.

These schools are no different than most high schools—populated as they are by a number of advisory groups, councils, or committees. Even with much specification about the role of each group, a principal is often hard-pressed to know which committees should be consulted. Consider the structure of relationships shown in Figure 1.1. Seven different advisory groups, likely with overlapping responsibilities, are available to the principal. A student discipline advisory council interacts with two others groups, but not the safe schools team. The technology committee appears to have no connections with other groups. What is the likelihood that great ideas get lost or morph into something entirely different as they travel from one group to another? How much time and energy do administrators expend trying to explain one advisory group's reasoning and evidence to another one?

> It is usually a bad idea to establish a special committee to investigate a problem.

Do the roles of the academic advisory council, site leadership team, and the shared leadership team overlap? Proposals likely get stuck between advisory groups or, worse yet, in an administrator's office. This structure for sharing leadership simply increases administrators' burdens and frustrates participants.

So what lessons can be extracted? A myriad of advisory groups with overlapping responsibilities and advice flow mostly through administrators and ensure that nothing much will happen. Marzano and his colleagues' (2001) case for shared leadership makes great sense to all school administrators, but clearly some ways of sharing leadership are more problematic than others.

Figure 1.1   Organization Chart for Anon High School

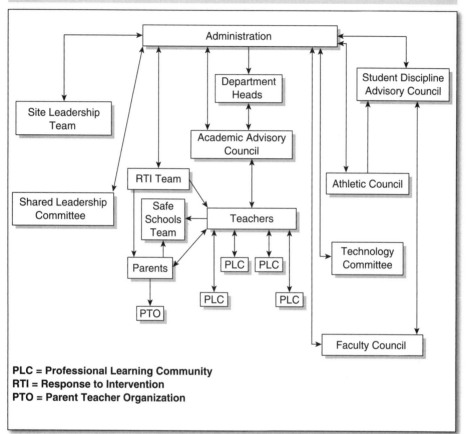

PLC = Professional Learning Community
RTI = Response to Intervention
PTO = Parent Teacher Organization

Case 2: Debilitating Processes

Most of us can remember where we were when the Columbia shuttle disaster occurred in 2003. We were nervous to learn that mission control had lost contact with the astronauts. As broadcasters reached for comforting explanations, Columbia debris scattered over Texas, Arkansas, and Louisiana. Finally, the dreadful and unexpected news: the Columbia shuttle had burst into flames on its re-entry into Earth's atmosphere. Rescuers found only shattered remains of the shuttle and its occupants.

Less well-known, much less remembered, is the fact that the *process* of making decisions contributed to this disaster. Much could have been done—possibly even a rescue—if the review process had been different. Transcripts show that conclusions were reached *before* evidence was explored—a process that blocked discovering alternatives.

In fact, James Surowiecki's (2004) investigation finds that staff engineers were quite concerned about the damage falling foam had done to the wings' tiles during liftoff. They initiated discussions with their supervisor about the risks involved and how they might acquire data to assess the risks and possible solutions.

As the shuttle circled Earth, team managers held a conference call—including the team leader for the engineers. As the conference call neared its end, the head manager asked the engineers' supervisor about possible damage to the tiles. He reported that the staff was hoping to have the opportunity to evaluate the situation. Neither the team leader nor others on the conference call asked any follow-up questions, such as how the engineers might complete such an evaluation. Instead, the team leader ended the exploration of the issue by saying: "I really don't think there is much we can do so it's really not a factor during the flight because there is not much we can do" (Surowiecki, 2004, p. 174). In fact, there were several things that could have been done.

The process for reviewing potential problems that led to the Columbia disaster not only eliminated evidence on the foam, but also obscured the organizational causes of potential problems. The board investigating the Columbia accident concluded:

> Many accident investigations make the same mistake in defining causes. They identify the widget that broke or malfunctioned, then locate the person most closely connected with the technical failure: the engineer who miscalculated an analysis, the operator who missed signals or pulled the wrong switches, the supervisor who failed to listen, or the manager who made bad decisions. When causal chains are limited to technical flaws and individual failures, the ensuing responses aimed at preventing a similar event in the future are equally limited: they aim to fix the technical problem and replace or

retrain the individual responsible. Such corrections lead to a misguided and potentially disastrous belief that the underlying problem has been solved. (Columbia Accident Investigation Board, 2003, p. 177)

Consider a school situation analogous to the Columbia disaster, but certainly with far less tragic results: a principal in a large suburban district convened a small group of teachers representing each grade level. He reported their superintendent's priority for the year to increase parent involvement in the district's schools. The principal presented his thoughts and proposed that each teacher have a minimum of one parent volunteer to assist in his or her classroom two times per week. When he asked for comments, suggestions, and concerns, one teacher inquired about how the parents would be recruited and trained. Another said she thought having more parent involvement would be "nice" but wondered if parents were really interested or had the time.

With no more discussion forthcoming, the principal concluded the meeting and sent out his expectations for increased parent involvement in the staff memo: The next school newsletter would include an invitation to parents to volunteer in classrooms. The parents should contact teachers if they could volunteer at least twice a week. The principal would track the number of volunteers with sign-in sheets submitted by each teacher.

While the prior experiences of some teachers surely prompted some enthusiasm for the proposal, others feared attracting only helicopter parents who would focus more on their own child's activities than the needs of other students or the teacher. From the principal's perspective, it was a productive meeting. He had a plan to address his superintendent's concern. He could check that task off his list. So, what happened next? Not much. The teachers waited for parents to respond to the newsletter. When parents failed to call, it confirmed the teachers' suspicions: parents are too busy or don't care to be involved.

Why did this plan fail? The meeting was organized and efficient, but it was not effective. The focus was clear. Yet, key elements needed to create a successful outcome were missing. The principal focused on achieving compliance rather than advancing school goals. Failing to seek out the buried wisdom in his staff, he lost the opportunity to assess how parent volunteers could contribute to school goals. More tragically, he reduced the level of energy and effort teachers applied to the task and increased the likelihood that teachers would keep good ideas to themselves.

It becomes obvious upon analysis why this effort and similar well-intentioned efforts—repeated daily in schools everywhere—cause frustration. To administrators, it reinforces their concern about sharing leadership. Teachers become more reluctant to share insights that might prove invaluable. Unfortunately such experiences also provide proof to teachers that "meetings are a waste of time, administrators don't listen, parents don't care, and this too shall pass."

Case 3: "Not My Problem" Fallacy

It's no surprise that many teachers think the last thing they need is another meeting—even if it is to ask their advice. Teachers want to attend to the challenges of creating powerful learning experiences for their students. However, the hard evidence on achieving excellence in education points to the need for educators to affirm the fundamental interdependency of their work (Bryk & Schneider, 2002).

Often, the depth of the interdependence is not obvious or so taken for granted that it's just an accepted part of the situation. Whether or not a teacher begins class with a room full of distressed students can be a function of what happened on the bus to school, the ugly or affectionate words in the hallway, or the tough exam in science.

The energy students apply to their work in any given class may be more a function of their accomplishments in the music room than the spellbinding story just read to them. A parent-teacher conference can be compromised by the frustration the parent experienced at the school's front office.

While special area teachers may be the most important resource for struggling students, they are seldom consulted. Teachers in mathematics may have developed some questioning strategies that could be useful in science classes, but science teachers will never

> **Student Life in a Middle School**
>
> "The good thing is that they have a lot of activities. The bad thing is that teachers don't pay much attention to what happens outside their classroom. If it happens outside their classroom, they don't care. It is not their problem."
>
> Reported on Great Schools website for a Florida school

learn about them. Perhaps educators could assist a struggling student if they had more information about available community resources. These are unrecognized interdependencies.

Reframing the way we organize schools begins by acknowledging the interdependence of a school's various parts and finding ways to exploit this interdependence. Student learning and well-being can only improve. We need to reframe the way we organize schools to improve information flow so that feedback reaches leaders more easily and encourages innovation to develop through informal networks.

While professional learning communities help educators increase their depth of understanding about the conceptual underpinnings of a subject and improve their instructional strategies, absent other structures or communication channels, schools will be unable to solve big problems. Any problem—student motivation, student truancy, or, say, postsecondary aspirations—has multiple causes and affects what teachers are able to accomplish in the classroom.

Organizational systems theorists emphasize that solving important problems requires multiple perspectives and seemingly diverse approaches to the solution. Ian Mitroff and Abraham Silvers (2010) find that lacking diverse perspectives, we often solve the wrong problem. They use the story of a manager for a high-rise office building who was receiving an increasing number of complaints about slow elevators. Engineering consultants proposed a complex solution limiting elevators to only a subset number of floors. The costs were staggering. A psychologist who worked in the building provided a different perspective: The wait time in this office building did not differ from others in the area. Working from theories about human behavior, she suggested they consider adding distracters in the lobby that would allow future passengers to occupy themselves—mirrored walls. It worked, and at much less cost. Many failures occur because we fail to acquire the multiple perspectives needed to solve the problem.

Case 4: Where's Help When You Need It?

Consider an interesting lesson from the military. As far back as the Civil War, medics saved many lives, but there were so many injured in their respective battalions that they were only able to save a small percentage of the soldiers needing help. Most of the injured soldiers bled to death before a medic arrived.

The most stunning reversal of the fates of many of America's youth in the military came when leaders realized that the most common cause of death could be reduced by preparing all soldiers to provide basic medical assistance: tourniquets. Increasing the number of people capable of providing relatively simple remedies in a timely manner to those injured likely saved many soldiers' lives in the past decade.

Tools and Imagination Can Save Lives

My son told me how wonderful the care packages we had sent them from the ladies auxiliary were and wanted me to tell everyone thank you. He said one guy got a female care package and everyone gave him a hard time. My son said, "Marine X got some really nice smelling lotion and everyone really likes it..." I told my son I was really sorry about the mistake and could send Marine X another package. He told me not to worry about Marine X because he shares my home-baked cookies with him.

Of course...there were those tampons. When he brought this up, my imagination just went running.

As they left one day on a mission, Marine X wanted the lip balm and lotion so he grabbed a bunch of the items from his care package and got in the Humvee. As luck would have it, he grabbed the tampons, too, and everyone teased him about "not forgetting his feminine hygiene products."

My son said things went well for a while, but then the convoy was ambushed. A Marine was shot. He said the wound was pretty clean, but it was deep. They were administering first aid but couldn't get the bleeding to slow down. Someone said, "Hey! Use X's tampons!" They put the tampon in the wound. "Mom, did you know that tampons expand?"

They successfully slowed the bleeding until the guy got better medical attention. "Mom, the tampons sent from the Marine Moms by mistake saved a Marine's life."

Anonymous Internet Story

Schools have come a long way in providing experts to support classroom instruction: many schools are staffed with literacy coaches, a parent involvement coordinator, and perhaps a technology coordinator. Incorporating new technologies or practices in classrooms, however, usually introduces simple problems that, unfortunately, require immediate attention. Proximity matters. When we introduced instructional management software to schools in the 1990s, one technology specialist devoted the vast majority of her time to assisting educators with basic computer skills (such as moving the cursor or accessing the server). It was impossible for her to respond in a timely manner to these needs. In schools, the adoption of new technologies or instructional approaches fails when the support needed to solve a simple problem is not available immediately.

The proximity of basic remedies for common glitches teachers experience with new tools or resources in the classroom is an essential part of reframing the support system within schools. Every team of educators—grade level, subject, or professional learning community—should have a person capable of "applying a tourniquet."

In the absence of coaches and coordinators, school administrators often fail to get help when it's needed and rely heavily on educators who volunteer to serve on advisory or support groups. Yet, such volunteers rarely distribute themselves evenly throughout the organization. Instead, volunteers for a data analysis team may be concentrated in the math department and the technology team comprised mostly of the science instructors. A history teacher hoping to learn to use a whiteboard may find that no one nearby knows anything about it. That is, unless he's got time to go to the science department, one floor or two wings away. Why should anyone be surprised when new technologies stand idle in the classroom?

Improving professional practice, then, requires attention to proximity. Some level of expertise needs to be embedded as close to the instructional challenges as possible. More than most professionals, the needs of educators are especially time sensitive. If connection to the Internet for the day's lesson fails, or is merely slow getting started, a wise teacher drops the plan immediately before chaos can emerge. Learning is lost and the time spent planning wasted.

Case 5: Schools as Pandas

Few animals are more vulnerable to shifts in their environment than pandas. They only eat *arrow* bamboo leaves; other types appear to be no substitute. In 2008, all the arrow bamboo in the panda's natural habitat began blooming—something that happens only once every 60 years. After they blossom, the plants wither and die. The bamboo does not grow for about 10 years. Pandas' inability (or unwillingness) to change to different sources of foods puts their future in doubt. The environmental shift in the supply of arrow bamboo is an externality that critically impinges on their future.

Schools demonstrate similar vulnerability shifts in their environment but for a different reason. Schools are vulnerable to changes in their environment because of their complexity. Schools must ensure the safety of large numbers of students and create meaningful learning experiences that address the needs of diverse students while maintaining compliance with various policies, regulations, and legislative mandates. The complex set of constraints created by bus schedules, extracurricular activities, or the management of a lunch schedule can make a simple shift in the "externalities" quite complex.

The environment in which schools operate changes constantly—perhaps due to a new superintendent, shifting academic standards, revised schedules for annual testing, a new remediation policy for those students failing to demonstrate proficiency on state assessments, or even natural disasters. The challenge is to find a process that can sensibly absorb the "shocks" that come from changes in their environment.

Analysts of school district issues rightly view schools as "part of the system" in their work. This is appropriate and likely even healthy. That said, from the point of view of a school in a large district, the adaptation is largely in one direction—schools adapting to district policies and decisions. School boards make decisions; state and federal legislators make laws. Schools do the adapting. If it were one system, with schools constituting subsystems, one would see *mutual* adaptation.

School adaptations to various shocks are no less likely than districts to solve the wrong problem. Worse yet, some strategies schools select can inadvertently undermine the essential goals or produce unanticipated consequences. For instance, a principal faced with a shift in school attendance boundaries chose a strategy for incorporating the new students and transferred teachers that had unanticipated consequences. In systems language, the new attendance boundaries were a "shock to the system"; that is, some external source was forcing an adaptation of "the way we do things around here." Hoping to make the students and parents comfortable in their new surroundings, the principal assigned all the teachers from the other school to students who attended that school. The parent-teacher association prepared a great welcome night for the new students, but the subsequent physical and social isolation reinforced the boundaries of the separate communities—encouraging rumors and misunderstandings. Clearly, this strategy failed to take into account all the issues.

Shocks to the system, or externalities, can be quite debilitating unless there are structures and processes for looking at the new situation from a variety of perspectives. Having structures in place that are ready and able to help adapt to the new policies or expectations coming from "outside" is essential. With various perspectives and expertise ready to support an administrator's decisions about how to adapt, the new ways of doing things can be transformative rather than debilitating.

Case 6: One Best Solution

It was clear to educators at this high school that student absenteeism was greatly compromising student learning and, consequently, the opportunities that students would have after graduation—presuming, of course, that they graduated. Even though their average daily attendance was almost 95 percent, 30 percent of students were absent more than 20 days in a given year. Knowing that parents cared about their children's performance—and even more about their future opportunities—it seemed like a no-brainer to get them involved in reducing absences.

The district's new management software allowed schools to establish a notification system—automatically calling parents in the morning if their child failed to appear in their first period class. Once operational, the educators saw only a slight improvement in student attendance. Even those statistics failed to reflect the experience of afternoon classes, where the low rate of attendance continued. Frustrated, school leaders called a special PTO meeting to discover other ways parents could encourage their children to attend school. Educators were thrilled by the large turnout of parents. They wrestled with additional incentives—such as awards for perfect attendance with weekly recognition for those with a perfect record. Awards and parents' interest brought enthusiasm, but little change.

While parental support and expectations are critical factors in high school students' attendance decisions, there are, in fact, multiple causes, some more important than others. Teachers know there are bright students who routinely skip classes. Are they working on projects for other classes? Are they just bored? What do we know about the incidences of "invisible" bullying—perhaps on the Internet or taunting after school? Tackling the problem of attendance requires that we begin with the assumption that there are multiple causes and likely all of them must be addressed to achieve a meaningful difference.

One of the reasons that the Mayo Clinic has such an extraordinarily high reputation as the place to go with life threatening illnesses is due to the way they organize the work of specialists. The clinic convenes a number of specialists (say, cardiology, pulmonary, and oncology specialists) to discuss a possible treatment regimen for a patient. Each brings a different perspective on the patient's symptoms or illnesses, the efficacy and dangers of certain treatment protocols, and the likelihood of success. For most of us, though, having a complex health problem rarely results in various specialists sitting down to discuss the issues. Instead, one specialist limits his diagnosis to those symptoms with which he is familiar. Just as success rates for seriously ill patients are higher when physicians collaborate to solve a patient's medical problems, so too with educators.

CONCLUSION

Identifying common problems in all types of organizations introduces us to the elements in the organization of professional life that require attention if we are to create a learning organization—an organization capable of transforming the quality of life and learning for everyone. If we want a school where educators create smart solutions to nagging problems, increase commitment to a school's best vision of its future, and gain satisfaction from meaningful improvements, we first need to adjust some structures and processes.

Schools with constipating organizational structures have ambiguous or overlapping roles and responsibilities. Communication channels are largely confined to links between administrators and advisory groups. Nothing changes in the way they do business because competing realities and solutions cannot be satisfactorily resolved—thus, the propensity to do nothing. Teachers' frustrations often lead to withdrawal from any advisory endeavors, since nothing ever happens.

Schools with poor processes for assessing problems often will fail to solve them. They may focus on compliance and miss opportunities to use new policies to solve existing problems. To the extent that the professional life in schools reinforces the myth that the challenges a school faces are "not my problem"—the quality of classroom instruction is diminished.

Successfully changing practices in organizations requires that needed information or expertise be in close proximity to those expected to make changes. Educators occupy one of the most time-sensitive roles found in any profession. Lacking quick support, they unlikely will be able to change how they organize classroom experiences for students.

Organizational structures need to allow schools to be proactive, rather than reactive, to the continuing influx of new policies and expectations. Proactive approaches allow educators to evaluate the implications from a variety of perspectives and to reduce the frequency of unanticipated problems that frustrate everyone.

Gaining, then, some appreciation for how professional lives in schools affect the quality of life experienced by both students and educators, we're ready to further investigate reframing a school's organization in ways that make everyone less frustrated and more successful in meeting the needs of students.

CHAPTER TWO

Essential Structure for Reframing Professional Life in Schools

We've gained some appreciation for how school structures and processes can generate frustration and mediocre outcomes. Now, we flip sides to establish guiding principles for what we need to reframe professional life capable of realizing the vision a school has for the students it serves.

We use the phrase "reframing professional life" to refer to explicit efforts to create or modify structures within an organization that create appropriate and useful flows of information, ensure that multiple perspectives and causalities are taken into account in solving problems, and, finally, enable schools to seamlessly adapt to frequent shocks.

What structural attributes of schools create the greatest capacity for adaptation? First, consider the flow of information: Does it flow in one direction or are there vibrant feedback loops that allow for adaptation and understanding? Does the structure foster cross-cutting ties across the organization? Second, is critical information (such as expertise in data analysis or instructional technology) spread across all formal and informal networks in the school? Does the process for decision making integrate not only instructional expertise of, say, department or grade-level coordinators, but also those general school conditions (such as culture and climate) that affect achievement?

INFORMATION FLOW

The flow of information—formal as well as informal channels of communication—affects the degree to which an administrator can understand the consequences of one action on a variety of other aspects of school life and the degree to which innovative solutions bubble up and are applied to vexing problems. The accuracy and frequency with which feedback arrives allows the administrator to assess how things are working and the ease with which the school will be able to convert shocks from the external environment into opportunities.

Representative membership: First and foremost, who is sitting at which table affects the flow of information, and thus the quality of advice and the ability to convert plans into a reality. A guiding coalition is a group of advisors that serves as a conduit for information to and from the formal and informal groups within an organization. While it would be easy to view this as a school's leadership team, we seldom see such teams populated in ways that could constitute a guiding coalition. First, in a guiding coalition, one must consider not only people with different perspectives and expertise, but also those educators with the capacity to mobilize an entire staff to support the goals they set, thus the need for informal leaders as well as those formally designated as such. Assembling a team of people who represent all dimensions of the organization—formal organizational units, informal social networks, and experts—allows a guiding coalition to consider all the possible effects that a given solution might have on the organization. Only then can a guiding coalition anticipate and prevent unintended consequences. As a system of interrelated parts, it becomes obvious that no one part stands independent of the rest—an underlying principle for reframing professional life in schools.

To obtain the best results, then, educators should begin by ensuring that a guiding coalition includes leaders from both the formal school structure as well as informal leaders; people with different perspectives, expertise, and levels of experience; and staff who can make a multiyear commitment. With those members at the table, a team has the opportunity to have a guiding coalition capable of making the best decisions.

Consider a case where multiple advantages emerged when one staff person joined a leadership team at a struggling middle school. Teachers were stunned when their principal (new to the school, but not the district) invited the worst curmudgeon in the building to join the guiding coalition. How could Ben Amos's grumpy approach to school life possibly be useful at the leadership team's summer organizational meeting? Ben's body language was negative, his input was minimal, and he left the meeting early. At the second meeting, he stated, "This group is a waste of time, because nothing ever changes at this school. We don't need more meetings, and we don't need more talk."

Why *did* the principal ask this person to be part of the team? This principal had visited Ben's classroom. He knew Ben was a strong instructor who cared about students, built working relationships with them, motivated them, engaged them in higher-order thinking, and energized otherwise struggling students. The principal often heard parents and other community members praise Ben's accomplishments and strong ties to the community.

Why was Ben so negative? Why were his colleagues unaware of his intense commitment to young people and effective teaching? Ben withdrew years earlier to protect himself and his energy. He was tired of all the rules, the talk, and the proposed changes of the past that failed to create meaningful and lasting impact. He was tired of attending meetings and struggling to affect the system. He had given up hope. He decided he was fighting a losing battle. So he closed his gate, buried his wisdom, and tended his tiny garden—the students in his classroom.

As a member of the guiding coalition, though, Ben's wisdom became apparent. His passion for teaching and learning guided his questions and concerns. Eventually, he became a guiding force for the team. He pushed the team to examine factors that impeded the real work of teachers. As the team began to address increasingly significant issues—and the guiding coalition, action teams, teachers, and administrators followed up appropriately—Ben lost his curmudgeon status. His positive and encouraging attitude infected his colleagues. Through Ben, a middle school administrator unleashed not just a better understanding of the school's challenges, but also a network of community leaders supporting the school's initiatives.

However, getting the right people on a guiding coalition is only the beginning. Developing expertise that can support the work of the various teams is essential—both in terms of the ability to garner wisdom from throughout the organization as well as the capacity to implement desired changes.

Diversity: A guiding coalition, as well as other school teams, must include different levels of expertise and experience. How does such a mix affect the quality of decisions? The initial clues emerged some 50 years ago as the military tried to understand how plane accidents happened in the absence of mechanical failures. As researchers (Levi, Torrance, & Pletts, 1955) reviewed the records of crews, including their training and experience, they were surprised to discover a pattern in the composition of the crews. In those avoidable accidents, the pilot was more likely to be the most experienced and highest ranking of the crew, the copilot the second most, and the navigator the newest and lowest ranking.

The patterns led them to conduct a series of experiments with flight simulations. What if crew statuses are mixed up? In fact, they found flight crews where the pilot was the youngest or lowest ranking, and the navigator, either the oldest or highest ranking, and so forth delivered more correct decisions than other crews. Status incongruities—it seems—made the crew more likely to offer their insights and the pilot more likely to listen carefully to the information and insight that other crew members offered. Fewer mistakes occurred, then, when a pilot was accompanied by a crew with more experience or rank. Subsequent studies of other organizations were consistent with these initial results.

James Surowiecki's (2004) more recent analysis of commercial flight disasters illustrates the dangerous mix of culture and structure. Extreme deference to authority led crew members to whisper their opinions (literally and figuratively) with disastrous results. Again, the wrong mix of expertise and experience led many to be reticent. The flight crew research reveals two critical insights about who is at the table: First, different perspectives, experiences, and training must be brought to the table before alternative actions are considered. Second, mixing ranks of team members increases the amount of wisdom that surfaces. The need to focus on "who's at the table" also emerges from John Kotter's (1996) research on organizational change. Making meaningful changes in practice, he concludes, requires a guiding coalition with respected representatives from every part of the organization—both in terms of formal responsibilities (departments, grade-level teams, support staff) as well as informal networks (experienced and less experienced staff, locals versus commuters, and so forth).

A guiding coalition and other teams will function most effectively when they are also composed of members with different thinking styles or temperaments. People who have different thinking styles often work well together, but they often fail to consider all of the possible concerns or solutions that come to light with a diverse group of thinkers. Given that the teams should be problem solvers, a diversity of styles is essential.

A guiding coalition enables a principal to have all the critical information and people available for review in one meeting. For the California high school described in Chapter 1, there was no *one* table but rather a myriad of diner booths that probably kept their principal dizzy with the constant stream of disparate ideas and solutions. While our victims of the constipated structure in Chapter 1 certainly provided administrators with advice, it's likely he received conflicting advice and frustrated his staff. A school administrator benefits from advisory groups only when they can evaluate the probable impact of one change on all aspects of school life. That's difficult, if not impossible, to do alone or even with other administrators.

A guiding coalition, however, only can do so much to reframe professional life and improve the quality of decisions. It is only the anchor for other structures and networks needed within a school. Other groups are needed to establish crosscutting ties, address the challenge of multiple causality, help absorb shocks to the system, and ensure greater proximity between a problem and a solution (the tourniquet).

Boundary spanners: A healthy, problem-solving organization requires that its members have relationships or connections across formal boundaries—departments, divisions, or grade levels. In small communities, many of these connections are established outside the school—in neighborhoods, churches or synagogues, or community clubs or organizations. While professional learning communities organized within subject areas or grades provide an essential foundation for invigorating instruction and increasing responsiveness to student needs, they seldom generate the crosscutting ties needed for teachers to acquire the larger context in which their work is positioned. Scholars who analyze human systems, such as Senge, argue that all members of an organization need an understanding of the big picture—the challenges and strengths in other parts of the organization.

The value of crosscutting ties, however, is not limited to "seeing the big picture," but also the opportunity to acquire innovative approaches not evident among the "like-minded" professionals in the same subject or grade level. Middle schools are most likely, we think, to begin solving this dilemma by having both grade-level and subject-area collaborations among teachers. This strategy broadens the view each educator has of the challenges, but other issues remain unaddressed—the opportunities for innovation, for instance, remain limited.

Proximity to need: Information flow also involves the degree to which those who know something are close to those who need to know it. Unlike our military, we too seldom have those tourniquets available when we need them. Innovation fails. Frustration and cynicism increase as a consequence.

Reframing a school's organization, then, requires that we ensure expertise is distributed evenly across our silos. In particular, basic skills in using new technologies as well as in data analysis should be evident in every department, grade level, or professional learning community.

ADDRESSING MULTIPLE CAUSALITY

School silos help educators to increase their depth of understanding, but absent other structures or communication channels, a school will be unable to solve big problems. Any problem—student motivation, student truancy, or levels of aspiration—has multiple causes. To solve the problem requires different perspectives and seemingly diverse approaches to the solution. Schools seldom have the structure and processes to look at their problem from a variety of angles. The challenge, then, is to reframe the professional structure in ways that help educators address problems from multiple perspectives.

Consider mathematics achievement. Real improvement may require reinforcing concepts in other academic disciplines as well as in helping parents to adopt more effective strategies for encouraging their children's efforts at school. Some students may need community service activities to acquire greater motivation to master mathematics.

In working with human systems, one best "solution" seldom, if ever, exists. Instead, any one problem has multiple causes—student absenteeism emerges not just from lack of parental oversight, but also from students' fear of failure, boring classes, scary hallways, taunting students, and, yes, illnesses. Addressing only one likely cause of absenteeism yields only meager results, at least when one is dealing with human behavior. Educators need to tackle the various causes simultaneously.

In meeting a school goal, leverage results when one focuses on the same goal and investigates multiple causality. Again, the meaning is best understood with its absence. Consider a school improvement plan: Student achievement in mathematics is flat and below the state's average. Professional development efforts focus on improving feedback strategies used by teachers. Parent involvement plans target increasing the attendance at PTO meetings. Business partners are asked to provide speakers at a career planning day. Acquiring clickers for the five teachers who requested them completes the school improvement checklist. Plans with such diverse targets inevitably dilute the impact on anything important. Any effect, for instance, that the career day has on students' motivation efforts in mathematics occurs by accident rather than design.

Leveraging refers to choosing actions or strategies that result in the biggest bang for the effort. In schools, leveraging occurs when educators tackle a problem in ways that address its multiple causes. In the previous example, leveraging was absent. Increasing PTO attendance is always good, but what's the likelihood that it will improve students' learning of mathematics? Some aspects of parent involvement are more likely to affect student learning than others. More important, changing some aspects of school life are more important than others. Michael Kirst and his colleagues (2006) in their study, *Similar Schools, Different Results,* find that schools serving a high proportion of students from low-income families can differ substantially in their achievement results. They found the higher achieving schools in their study were much more likely than low achieving to

- focus on ensuring a coherent, standards-based curriculum;
- encourage teacher collaboration;
- enforce high expectations for student behavior;
- use assessment data to improve student learning;
- ensure the availability of instructional resources;
- prioritize student achievement; and
- involve and support parents.

The schools with the most profound improvement in student learning, however, were those schools that effectively addressed *all* these elements. If these are core issues, which we think they are, then we have an initial cut at how to frame our investigation of multiple causality. That is, for any given problem, a school should have ways to evaluate how each of the areas identified by Kirst and his colleagues may be part of the solution to a problem a school seeks to address.

PROVIDING SHOCK ABSORBERS

Anticipating, rather than reacting to, change requires that schools review new state or district policies or expectations in terms of the needed adjustments and/or possible opportunities in all of the critical areas identified previously. Unlike biological systems, human social systems have much more adaptive capacity than other types of systems simply because people can be active creators of the systems they inhabit. Humans create or change structures (roles and relationships) and processes for executing tasks (monitoring what is working) in the systems they inhabit. If the equivalent of phosphate fertilizer creeps into our school, within certain ranges, we can find ways to make it useful or get it out of there. Yet all too often, we unwittingly allow such shocks to extinguish valuable parts of school life. We sometimes choose to eliminate recesses to capture more time for improving reading comprehension. We may drop quick checks for understanding in order to stay on track with a pacing guide. Interdisciplinary units may be abandoned because they seemingly fail to contribute to performance on state assessments. Yet one or more of these decisions reduce the ability of a school to improve student learning and performance.

REFRAMING PROFESSIONAL LIFE

Understanding what's needed for systems thinking to emerge, we're prepared to consider what types of structures and processes we need to create. Systems thinking is not new to educators. The notion of reframing professional life is new—at least in ways we propose to think about it. That said, we begin with a definition of systems and those aspects of system analysis or thinking that we consider crucial to this work.

In its most general sense, a system is a set of interrelated parts that interact to achieve a goal. A mechanical system, like a thermostat, is designed with one "goal"—ensuring that a room maintains a temperature set by an external agent (you or me). It has a sensor—one part of the system—that triggers either a heating or cooling subsystem to turn on when the temperature goal is not met. The sensor represents an essential part of all systems: *feedback* mechanisms. Actual room temperature provides the feedback. Humans, not part of the thermostat system, set its goals. We don't like the goal; we change it. Feedback mechanisms are just one part of a larger concept—information flow—that will be essential in our thinking about schools as systems.

Peter Senge and colleague's (2000) landmark field book for educators, *Schools that Learn*, provides a wealth of illustrations of the interdependencies that exist within districts and schools. It is designed to help educators address barriers to team building, such as the mental models that limit how individuals can look at a problem, or how the level of trust among team members affects the willingness to confront delicate, but important, issues. Yet, no attention is given to the types of communication channels needed for transformations to occur or how educators can best organize to identify multiple causes of the problems they face.

The application of Senge's approach, along with that of W. Edwards Deming and Mary Walton in 1988, to improving schools' education relies upon episodic groupings of like-minded educators working to solve a given problem. Too often, however, the groups generate few changes. Enthusiastic reformers often become disheartened—either because their groups, sometimes called *quality circles*, became just another forum for complaining or another verification that the administration really doesn't want to listen to their recommendations.

Newmann and his colleagues' (2001) research on school improvement efforts in urban schools reminds us of the other persistent weaknesses of such episodic teams in schools. In their study of urban schools, administrators typically relied on ad hoc committees to focus on specific initiatives or newly adopted programs. "They devote a great deal of time and energy into multiple workshops, meetings, and conferences. . . . With time, desired improvements in student achievement gains fail to materialize and professional fatigue and frustration rise. Many of these improvement programs fade, or end, while new programs continue to be adopted" (Newmann, Smith, Allensworth, & Bryk, 2001, p. 298). Frustration and disillusionment inevitably follow the demise of a specific program; expertise gained in the effort gets lost as new programs are adopted. The structural flaws of quality circles and ad hoc committees overwhelm any useful process developed within them.

Fortunately, reframing a school's organization to incorporate the structure and processes needed to address the issues of information flow, multiple causality, and shocks to the system is not as complex as it might seem. The task is to overlay the professional working groups focused on improving instruction with teams that are focused on schoolwide issues.

As we will stress several times, the fundamentals lie with the composition of those teams focused on schoolwide goals. In some instances, merging, converting, or expanding existing advisory groups, such as those focused on school discipline, will be needed.

We need a structure that allows schools to work smarter. Rather than adding teams and committees to an already cluttered picture, we provide a strategy for consolidating existing groups into teams to address core issues. The leadership team is the guiding coalition that links directly to six action teams whose membership includes one or more representatives from each grade level or department.

Figure 2.1 identifies the teams needed to reframe schoolwide efforts. First, note that the action teams link departments' grade-level teams in the school. Each department has at least one member on each action team—establishing a baseline for diverse perspectives and the creation of boundary spanners. Second, the chair of each action team is also a member of the guiding coalition—serving as a conduit in both directions. Action teams support core issues: curriculum and instruction, technology, professional development, school culture and climate, data analysis, and parent and community partnerships. This framework ensures that multiple causes of any one problem can be assessed. Over time, each action team develops expertise in one core issue—an expertise that the guiding coalition relies upon for advice about resolving problems and support in implementing new activities. Through the same structure, grade-level or department teams have easy access to needed expertise, especially in technology and data analysis.

Thus, the decision to focus on core issues, rather than specific projects or programs, increases the likelihood that an effective team is ready to help with new issues in their focus area. Their acquired expertise can help the school assess the potential of other programs, and grade-level teams or departments have one or more resource persons in each of the core areas. When grade-level teams or department members meet, their increased ability to understand the breadth of perspectives on school issues reduces the likelihood that seemingly minor decisions create problems for other parts of the organization.

The guiding coalition ensures that proposals from the action teams advance schoolwide goals with implementation schedules that complement rather than compete with each other. The coalition monitors the progress of each action team and encourages adjustments as data may dictate. They help celebrate action team accomplishments and conduct an annual debriefing on the school initiatives to help improve future schoolwide efforts.

When schools begin to reframe their organization, they should work to convert or incorporate existing advisory groups (such as one in technology) or response-to-intervention committee into an action team. In so doing, however, they should expand their membership to ensure that they include members from every formal unit (grade-level team, professional learning communities, or department) of the school staff. Over time, this

Figure 2.1 Organizational Structure for Systems Leadership

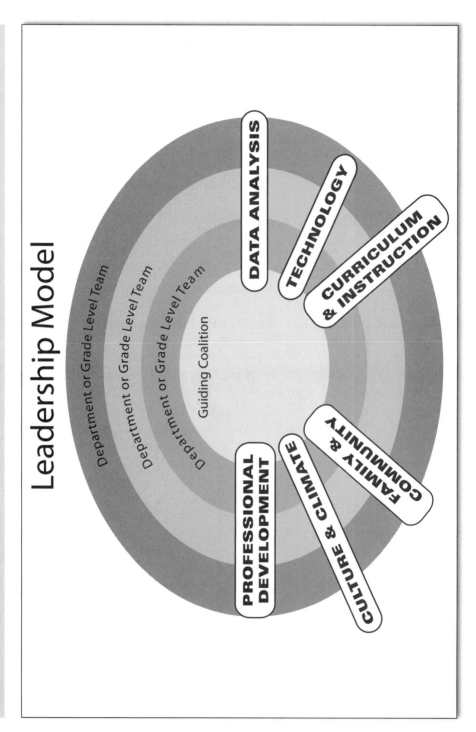

Leadership Model

Department or Grade Level Team

Department or Grade Level Team

Department or Grade Level Team

Guiding Coalition

DATA ANALYSIS

TECHNOLOGY

CURRICULUM & INSTRUCTION

PROFESSIONAL DEVELOPMENT

CULTURE & CLIMATE

FAMILY & COMMUNITY

structure will distribute expertise across all sectors of the school, encourage innovation through the new networks among staff, and increase the staff's understanding of the various initiatives within the school.

Another final note: A Technology Action Team is helpful if it is full of computer wizards, but it will have critical weaknesses. Team members lacking wizard wands will be invaluable as advisors on acquisitions or strategies for broad adoptions of new technology.

CONCLUSION

Reframing professional life provides a way to organize collaborative efforts around persistent challenges or enduring needs. It allows information and recommendations to flow systematically to a guiding coalition (i.e., the leadership team). A clear focus on schoolwide goals enhances the ability to realize substantial improvements by addressing multiple domains. Ultimately, it changes the way people approach and discuss issues and allows the processes for continuous improvement to become integrated into the routines of school life.

CHAPTER THREE

Essential Processes for Teamwork

Having the appropriate mix of people on teams and connecting them coherently is a necessary condition for successfully reframing an organization, but it's hardly sufficient. How work gets done will greatly affect the success of any team. All too often, committee meetings are on educators' lists of bad experiences. Educators stand in good company with people in all types of organizations. While some teams or committees generate exceptionally smart solutions to problems that no one person could have developed, others wallow in small talk and haphazardly adopt the easiest action or remedy proposed. It's a paradox, but researchers find that the best and worst decisions arise from group deliberations. Unfortunately, the bad decisions and frustrating processes encourage leaders to limit group consultations.

But why do the outcomes vary so radically? In simple terms, superior versus mediocre results from group deliberations rest on two factors: who's at the table (discussed in Chapter 2), and how they do their work. In this chapter, we identify the processes teams need to follow for their work to create superior results.

We discuss the process of alignment both within and across teams. This includes the need to maintain focus on those conditions that are within a school's circle of influence, the importance of establishing norms for group discussions and decisions, how using evidence helps frame the problem and evaluate possible solutions, and the value of looking at school processes—rather than individual challenges—as the source of problems.

HOW DO SUCCESSFUL GROUPS DO THEIR WORK?

Achieve Alignment

The lack of alignment among people, teams, and programs leads to inertia and confusion. Alignment begins with a vision and short-term goals shared by all. A vision statement points to where an organization wants to be within a specified period. A goal states a meaningful step toward that vision.

Alignment exists when all teams and individual members on the teams address the same goal in a committed, systematic, and organized way. Without alignment, energy is wasted as they "bump into" each other. The harder they work, the more frustration mounts because the desired results are not accomplished.

Lacking alignment, the discussions may look something like Figure 3.1.

Figure 3.1   Lack of Alignment Within a Team

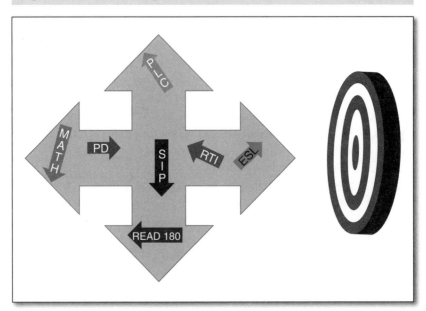

When individuals are in alignment, however, their energy works to propel them and others toward the common vision and the immediate goal. As Peter Senge (1990) explains, "In fact, alignment is the necessary condition before empowering the individual will empower the whole team. Empowering the individual when there is a relatively low level of alignment worsens the chaos and makes managing the team even more difficult" (p. 235). For a team to be in alignment, the members must agree on the goals they are pursuing. Common purpose begins to strengthen the commitment and energy necessary to move forward. Next, the team must learn to work together in ways that strengthen the team's capacity to produce results. Putting people on a team does not mean they will be able to work together. Without common purpose and a clear process for working together, they are simply a bunch of individuals "bumping into each other's assumptions, ideas and actions" (p. 235).

With alignment, everyone is pulling in the same direction—toward a clearly stated goal (see Figure 3.2). The members have an understanding of how to complement one another's actions and efforts. Educators make use of all the school's resources to achieve their goals. That's coherence. The laserlike focus of people and their energies on the same goal is fundamental to creating this synergy among group members and ultimately within the entire system. Action is clearly linked to attaining the goal. All efforts of the group support the expected results embedded within the goal. The group is clear about what actions will detract from attaining the goal. When policies or other activities conflict or undermine a goal, the guiding coalition must consider how they might be changed or eliminated.

Figure 3.2   Alignment Within a Team

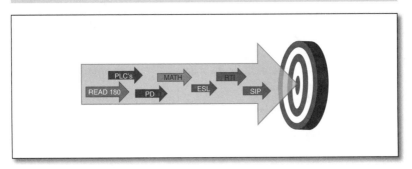

In a comprehensive study of teams, J. Richard Hackman (2005) of Harvard University argues that a leader is responsible for creating this clarity. "Teams need a compelling direction. Unless a leader articulates a clear direction, there is a real risk that different members will pursue different agendas" (p. 123). Pursuing different agendas is not effective. Alignment begins with the guiding coalition and works its way into the action teams as a shared vision and goal.

Everyone Was Committed, but Only Frustration Emerged

A teacher-leader had led a number of committees in the past, and he felt confident in leading this one. Teachers had volunteered from across the district to work on a new discipline policy. To use time efficiently, he asked them to read the current policy prior to the first meeting and come prepared with suggestions for changing and improving it. At the first meeting, they brainstormed ideas and made a list of suggestions. People left the meeting frustrated and lacking enthusiasm for the next meeting. But, they weren't sure exactly why they felt that way. The leader felt frustration also and even a sense of resistance among the group. What was missing?

If people volunteered, they should be interested and committed to the goal. But what was the goal? Why did they need a new policy? What did the data say? What was the current situation? What were the legal guidelines? Was the current policy working in some schools? Why was each person attracted to this committee? What background and interests did each one bring that could be helpful here? What were the ground rules for the group? What were the decision-making criteria? These are questions that required answers before the committee could achieve alignment.

By not taking time to clarify the issues and process that would create the alignment of the people within the group, the members had no structure for working together. Without that foundation and alignment of people, purpose and process, the group was left without the ability to build the skills and capacity of the members to create the alignment of energy and action.

Focus on Issues Within One's Circle of Influence

A team must begin by realistically defining its circle of influence. Groups get stuck when they spend time on challenges outside their circle of influence. If team members in a school constantly raise concerns about the federal mandates, new state regulations, or their district's switch to a new mathematics text, they share their concerns but accomplish very little. These conditions are outside their circle of influence. Regular meetings with committed individuals focusing on legitimate (or not so legitimate) concerns that they cannot influence lead nowhere.

Members of such unproductive teams begin bringing papers to grade and magazines to peruse during the meetings. The team members are most likely to describe their team meetings as "negative," "repetitive," "boring," or "a waste of time." Clearly, such teams are stuck in a rut. If teams spend their meeting time blaming parents, disagreeing with school board policies, or railing against federal laws they feel are obstacles to their effectiveness, then convening meetings is indeed a waste of time. Their perceptions may be correct; their concerns may be appropriate. Addressing the perceptions and concerns, however, requires different people at the table—and even a different table.

The purpose of the team is to solve problems and remove obstacles that decrease the effectiveness of the teachers and compromise student learning. That said, not just any problem can be addressed. Stephen Covey (1990) in his classic work, *The 7 Habits of Highly Effective People,* argues that one of the keys to any team's effectiveness is its ability to spend time and energy on issues, ideas, and actions that are within its circle of influence. That is, issues on which the team can have an impact.

Teams are more likely to focus on the right issues when they begin by describing the differences between their circle of *concern* and their circle of *influence*. Within their circle of concern might be the state's raising the benchmark for proficiency in mathematics or the reduction of paid professional development days. While these are areas of legitimate concern for some entity to address, they are not issues that reasonably can be addressed by a school-based team; that is, these issues are outside their circle of influence. Each team should clarify its own boundaries—identifying those issues that actually can be addressed and agreeing to redirect or discontinue conversations that lead the team into the "wilderness of no influence." In the case of raising state benchmarks, the issue can be reframed within the group's circle of influence by focusing on what changes the school and teachers can make to ensure that students reach those new benchmarks.

Reframing professional life to create an adaptive system begins with a common focus for all teams. Suppose the focus is on the low performance on the state mathematics assessment. Teams clarify their boundaries by having team members identify which barriers need to be addressed to solve the problem. After all members individually explain what they perceive to be the barriers, the team discusses and agrees on whether each fits within the circle of influence or that of the circle of concern.

Obviously, one group cannot address all of these at one time. That is one reason why the effort to reframe professional life in schools can be so valuable. Different action teams, which we will introduce later in this section, may address one of these questions and determine what issues are within its circle of influence (see Figure 3.3).

Establish Group Norms

In addition to focus and alignment, successful groups have explicit guidelines—or norms—that set expectations for how the group works together. These guidelines enable the individuals to listen for understanding and seek clarity in a respectful environment.

Respectful communication begins with an appreciation of the fact that what we hear may not always be what was said. In seeking to clarify a proposal, participants refrain from shock and awe. Genuine respect for others' professionalism allows us to maintain some humility regarding our understanding of other people's points of view. Establishing norms allows members to agree upon how they will listen and verify.

Equally important, respect and trust allow participants to approach conflicting data as a curiosity to be questioned, explored and resolved, rather than—to take the extreme case—the opening round of a personal conflict. Collins (2001) in his work, *Good to Great*, argues that "A primary task in taking [an organization] from good to great is to create a culture wherein people have a tremendous opportunity to be heard, and, ultimately, for the truth

Figure 3.3   Focusing on Problems Within One's Circle of Influence

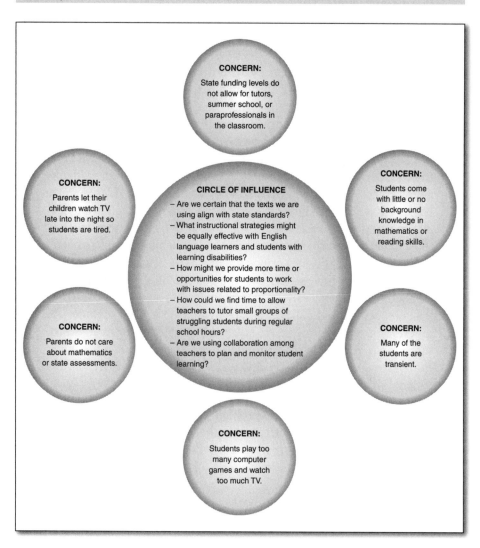

to be heard" (p. 88). Conflicting evidence is an opportunity, not a challenge. Hearing others is a process *and* an attitude.

To be effective, the group norms must be simple, developed with input from the group, and followed by all participants. Establishing these group guidelines at the beginning of the group's formation is preferred. However, it is never too late for an established group to have the conversation to create its norms. Commonly adopted team norms are shown in Table 3.1.

Begin With the Evidence

Great decisions occur only when information gathering precedes conclusions. In the Columbia disaster, evidence was not even sought, much less reviewed. While the Columbia disaster was the result of failing to examine evidence altogether, the more common mistake is using limited evidence to solve the wrong problem.

Suppose a school needs to address disciplinary problems with their students. Before reasonable solutions can be posed, evidence needs to be evaluated. For instance, are certain students more likely to have disciplinary problems than others? Which grade levels or ethnic groups seem most affected? When and where are they most likely to occur? Has the incidence of discipline problems been constant over the past several years or is it increasing? What types of interventions have we used in the past? What does research tell us about the efficacy of various strategies to resolve this problem? All perspectives and data need to be available for team members to digest. Not unlike a mystery novel, as the story moves forward, teams should be able to eliminate some suspects but not others; that is, some explanations and solutions become more or less salient as the evidence accumulates.

Context: Before analyzing any problem or addressing any goal, educators should always investigate whether the needs of the students and parents they serve are changing. Looking at data without a

Table 3.1   Commonly Adopted Team Norms

- Meetings begin and end on time.
- Everyone participates.
- Members turn off their cell phones.
- Everyone listens respectfully.
- Members do not conduct sidebar conversations.
- Members problem solve, not blame.
- Silence assumes consent.
- Members focus on what they can influence.

context is meaningless (Deming & Walton, 1988). A grocery store can go out of business not because of its poor processes, such as good consumer relations, but because a manager fails to adjust what's on the shelves to meet the needs of changing demographics. An influx of new neighborhood residents with more or less money to spend on groceries may make the products too expensive or undesirable to potential customers.

School demographics and family conditions also change. What had been effective in one context may not be in another one. In the 1990s, changes in welfare regulations affected the degree to which some mothers were available to help at school. Some schools were slow to realize why many moms were not available to participate in school activities. Working harder on the same things would not have made a difference.

> **Spurious Correlations**
>
> In remote islands of the South Pacific, people traditionally treated high fevers by putting lice in hair. Why? They noticed that persons with a high fever *lacked* hair lice; all those without a fever *had* hair lice. They concluded that it was the absence of lice that caused the fever. In fact, though, it was the fever that caused the lice to leave the hair of the patient! Even lice flee hot places.

Comparisons: Comparing the problems one is attempting to resolve with those of similar schools or districts helps narrow the possible causes one should evaluate. For instance, suppose your school experiences a dramatic drop in student performance on eighth-grade mathematics assessments from the previous year. Did that occur districtwide? Did similar schools experience a similar drop in performance?

If the answer is yes, then the problem of alignment between what is taught and what is assessed is a more likely cause than the instructional strategies at your school. Looking closer at your own data, if you find that students in all subgroups experienced the drop in performance, then that initial suspicion has greater credibility. It makes no sense, at least initially, to focus on improving instructional strategies until the alignment between what is taught and what is assessed is evaluated. Such problems can emerge with a new testing regime or standards, or the adoption of a new text.

While it may be tempting to consider such a lack of alignment outside a school's circle of influence, it is only the cause that is outside of its influence. Educators can generate solutions in their schools as well as communicate with critical decision makers.

If, on the other hand, such comparisons show that the problem is unique to your school, then the challenge is to dig deeper into school practices to understand why the dip in performance occurred.

Trends: Identifying possible causes of problems that seem fairly unique to a school requires acquiring an understanding of the problem over time. For instance, looking at academic performance issues over time will help determine if one should address a cohort problem or a grade-level problem. A cohort problem refers to a change in performance or behavior that is specific to a group of students. A cohort issue exists if, say, sixth graders in 2007 demonstrated the same problem as eighth graders in 2009. Educators often tag a cohort with "just that group of students"—sometimes viewed with amusement, other times with alarm. Focusing on the poor performance in reading in the eighth grade without looking at such trends may lead to solving the wrong problem.

Subgroup analysis is an important component of trend analysis. Sometimes the poor performance of, for example, fifth-grade Latinos may not originate in the fifth grade, but rather in earlier grades. The problem becomes apparent only in the fifth grade, perhaps because of the shift in the importance (i.e., the number of assessment items) of one skill over another.

Consider Process Issues First

William Edwards Deming, an organization and systems guru of the 1960s and 70s, worked from the assumption that individuals are inherently motivated to do a good job. As a consultant, he observed that most organizational problems emerge from the system, that is, the way they are organized. In particular, he urged leaders to look at processes used to manufacture a product or achieve a goal. He insisted that the *ways* we do things at work (rather than the *people* that do the work) are the source of most organizational issues. American industries largely ignored Deming's work until Japanese auto companies (thanks to Deming's advice) began producing far more superior products than their American counterparts (Ouichi, 1983).

One simple contrast of earlier practices has an interesting parallel in education. American automakers of the 1960s and 70s undertook a quality review of their newly minted cars at the end of the production line—after everything was put together. With Deming's counsel, Japanese automakers initiated quality reviews at every stage of production. The result was better cars at lower prices (Deming & Walton, 1988). A change in the process changed results. The availability of formative and interim assessments in schools, supplementing teachers' routine diagnostics, allows students' learning problems to be resolved earlier with much greater success and much less frustration.

Consider this case: High school teachers were frustrated. Each week it seemed like more students were arriving late to their first period classes. Data showed that the problem did not occur with other periods in the day. Yet, a sudden change in students' sleeping habits or parents' commitment to education seemed unlikely. Changing penalties for tardiness to address not only if the student was late for class, but also how late, would be complicated. Perhaps they should offer rewards for being on time or intensify disciplinary procedures. At a staff meeting, however, a department chairwoman asked, "Do we have some new procedures for buses, breakfast, or processing students who arrive late that could account for this situation?"

A highly conscientious new assistant principal began to explain how she had changed the processing of students arriving late in the morning. Students must go to her office rather than to the school's secretary. It provided her, she explained, with the opportunity to get to know the students who were having difficulty getting to school on time. Her conscientious behavior, however, easily added 15 minutes to the process. It was, in Deming's mind, a question of process.

When seeking the root cause of problems, wise teams look for those organizational processes that may be contributing to the challenge. When a team limits possible explanations of problems to a lack of training or negligence, the best solutions may be overlooked.

Looking at Processes Can Yield Simple Solutions

Otherwise well-behaved students baffled teachers at this middle school. Students gathered in the gym before school. The trash left behind was enormous and certainly not consistent with their ability to get cafeteria and classroom trash into a receptacle. Why was the gym always a disaster zone? One teacher thought to ask some of her students: Why the mess? With some probing, the teacher discovered that the location of the trash bin required students to walk across the front of the bleachers where other students were sitting. Fearing some type of embarrassment (falling down or dropping something), students chose to leave trash around where they sat rather than risk such trauma. One day later, the trash cans were repositioned at the top of the bleachers, and within a couple of weeks, most students took a more or less invisible walk to the receptacle. Trash largely disappeared from the bleachers.

CONCLUSION

Nearly all educators enter the profession with a passion for teaching and making a difference in young people's lives. The way we live out our lives in schools, though, leaves many of us wondering if the routines and policies we live with reflect that priority. Reframing professional life can help educators realign their energies and focus on addressing those fundamental passions.

The processes educators use in their collaborative efforts will make a difference. When efforts focus within the school's circle of influence, alignment of purpose exists within and across teams, norms of discourse reflect professional relations, deliberations begin with evidence and focus on process-oriented solutions, and educators will experience not only satisfaction, but results.

Getting the right people at the table and following productive processes mobilizes naturally occurring social networks and builds a broad base of trust that can facilitate risk taking (Bryk & Schneider, 2002). Over time, the expertise educators acquire allows easy diffusion of ideas and solutions across grades and subjects and secures continued improvement of practice through professional learning communities within each grade-level team or department.

CHAPTER FOUR

Managing Change Successfully

C hanges in priorities and practices are an inevitable part of any profession. Yet as one acquires more experience as an educator, one risks acquiring a measure of cynicism: promising new practices look more like old ideas in new packaging. If it didn't work then, why should it now? Educators, particularly in urban areas, face the prospect that the new solution will be abandoned whenever the visionary leaves. Why risk being stuck with an orphaned vision? Just waiting it out seems fairly sensible. We all want things to be better—especially for our students—but sometimes less change may be the best route.

Ideas from "afar" require special suspicion: How do we know it will work with our students? Is it truly appropriate for my grade? Were they working with standards similar to those we have in our state? These are valid questions.

More important, though, significant changes in practice for any profession bring frustration, as one's effectiveness usually gets worse before it gets better. Even with the best guidance, a teacher confronts instances where instructions were vague, students became confused, or equipment didn't work as promised. Every teacher knows even small glitches can sink a new instructional program, strategy for taking attendance, or lunch schedule.

When we change instructional materials—be it textbooks or software—we don't feel productive. In fact, with new ways of doing things we usually are not as productive in the beginning. Economists have a name for the problem: sunk costs. For instance, for every additional year we use a particular tool—such as presentation software—we become better at using it. Using whiteboards may prove, in the end, to be better. Before that happens, though, one has to invest time in developing new supporting materials, reframing student participation strategies, becoming comfortable with a new set of buttons, and learning new ways of walking and talking. The time invested mastering some software constitutes the sunk costs not recovered when replacing that technology with a new one.

More subtle challenges arise when norms—accepted ways of doing things—change. Suppose a principal adopts a new policy welcoming parents into classrooms at any time: How will a teacher manage the disruptions parents may create? How much time will it take to welcome them and possibly even make them useful to classroom instruction? Or, perhaps a department chair or principal proposes sessions where teachers discusses students' work: Will teachers feel uncomfortable as colleagues discuss their student assignments? In both of these examples, norms shift and may require reframing relationships while maintaining or creating trust. New senses of vulnerability can emerge.

In this chapter we discuss the conditions that make some changes in practice more drastic and challenging than others, and what researchers find as the requisite steps for successful change.

WHAT WE KNOW ABOUT CHANGING ORGANIZATIONS AND INDIVIDUALS

Some change is harder than others: In Waters, Marzano, and McNulty's (2003) discussion of improving schools, they distinguish between first and second order changes. First order changes are those that are an extension of the past, will function within existing paradigms and prevailing values and norms, and are focused, bounded, and incremental. As Luc de Brabandere (2005) frames it: first order change "is produced within a system that stays the same. If it modifies a component it still follows the same rules" (p. 6). Hence, the famous claim, "The more something changes, the more it stays the same."

Second order changes are those that break with the past, work outside the existing paradigm and values, and are emergent, unbounded, and complex. For this to occur, at least one of the rules of the system—an assumption, a stereotype, or an implied priority—must also change (de Brabandere, 2005). Second order changes are tougher because most people will need to learn new approaches to routine tasks, with the risk of stumbling through the new way of doing things. Tougher still, they may need to resolve inherent challenges to their assumptions or values.

Consider these examples: Among the essential roles in education leadership, Waters, Marzano, and McNulty (2003) find student achievement is higher when leaders recognize school accomplishments and acknowledge failures. A first order change addressing this issue occurs when a school leader institutes ways to acknowledge accomplishments. This should require little, if any, challenge to values or paradigms held by staff members. Complexity is also absent: a box of note cards may be all that is needed to begin. On the other hand, acknowledging school failures can challenge existing norms and values—perhaps the unspoken assumption the principal is "always right" or a norm of privacy of practice among teachers. A principal's open admission that the lunchroom policy was not working well for teachers and students, for instance, could make some staff members wonder about her authority while others might gain new respect for her honesty.

In schools, even first order changes in school practice can be complex. Extending the school day for some children (allowing for additional tutorial time for struggling readers, for instance) may be consistent with existing values and assumptions, but require negotiating bus driver schedules, teacher responsibilities, and janitorial duties, to name a few.

Developing a foundation of trust can be complex, yet necessary, if staff is to discuss school problems openly and productively. Anthony Bryk and Barbara Schneider (2002), in their study of Chicago schools, found that trust among teachers, between teachers and the principal, between teachers and parents, and between students and teachers, are important preconditions for creating a positive orientation toward change and actual improvements in student engagement and learning. In particular, teachers need to believe a principal respects their professionalism and point of view. Without that, little substantive change can occur.

Individual change requires change in action and perception: To push the challenge further, de Brabandere (2005) explains: "Any individual change that makes a difference requires a person change twice. You not only need to change the reality of your situation, you also needs to change your *perception* of this reality" (p. 7). Said another way, an individual encounters two levels of change: first, one must change routine ways of doing things, and second, how one *perceives* the changes.

For example, teachers can change an instructional practice, perhaps introducing graphic organizers. Unless they understand the value of using graphic organizers in the context of student learning, however, teachers' decisions to use the technique will be driven mostly by convenience and fail to create a change in outcome. On the other hand, when a teacher understands how a graphic organizer complements the way our brain works (that is, it improves a student's conceptual understanding and greatly increases retention), the tool becomes potent and generates results. The teacher's understanding of the tool leads to changed perceptions—a different understanding of the value of the tool—and only then can one realize a meaningful change in practice. Rather than just adding an additional strategy to a long list of miscellaneous options, the perceptions of graphic organizers changes the *way* one teaches. Graphic organizers affect how the teacher thinks, plans, and presents. Thus, in this case, understanding how a practice is connected to learning, the why of it all, creates a change that is not only self-sustaining, but also more effective.

Develop shock absorbers: So how do schools avoid "the panda effect," that is, being vulnerable to changes in their environment as described in Chapter 1? Said another way, how do schools increase the ability of educators to adapt to the ever emerging "panda shocks" associated with changes in district policies, state accountability systems, or federal regulations change?

William Ouchi (1983), in his classic comparison of Japanese and American automobile makers in the 1970s, gives us some clues. American executives quickly made offers for new partnerships. Japanese executives, on the other hand, seemed to take an interminable amount of time making a decision. When the agreement was finalized, however, the Japanese company moved seamlessly into implementation while the American company sputtered and delayed. The difference? In Japan, executives had consulted with engineers, floor workers, and quality control engineers—in fact, every group that might be affected—*before* they signed on to the partnership. They were asked what needed to be done for the proposed partnership to work. In contrast, American executives had consulted no one and learned only after the fact that the agreement required shifts in procedures and processes to work effectively.

When policies or expectations are changing, action teams prove critical to a smooth transition. They, along with administrators, can identify the adjustments that will be needed to ensure success. The school, then, does not merely anticipate a change, but secures insight about needed adjustments from a variety of perspectives. Once plans for adjustments are complete, all action teams have a role in implementing them.

STEPS FOR SUCCESSFUL CHANGE

John Kotter (1996) spent over 20 years watching hundreds of companies engage in second order changes. These included manufacturing plants and hospitals that were on the verge of closing as well as schools and communications companies that were underperforming and attempting to remake themselves. The more people in the organization understood the change needed, the more effectively the change was implemented. Kotter also found changes in behavior occur more often when leaders speak to people's core values.

Successful processes for instituting a major change, Kotter concludes, consistently follow eight phases that "create power and motivation sufficient to overwhelm all the sources of inertia" (p. 20). The first four steps "help defrost a hardened status quo" (p. 22). The remaining steps move the organization toward its vision.

Steps For Successful Change

1. Establish a guiding coalition.
2. Create a sense of urgency.
3. Get the vision and strategy right.
4. Secure buy-in.
5. Empower staff.
6. Get short-term wins.
7. Consolidate gains and expand scope of effort.
8. Make it stick.

Adapted from Kotter, 1996

Establish a guiding coalition: We trust the notion of a guiding coalition seems familiar. For, as noted in Chapter 2, organizing for success begins with identifying a guiding coalition that brings staff with a diverse set of experiences and expertise to the table. As respected members of all parts of the organization and informal networks, the guiding coalition provides insight into the challenges and can help their colleagues understand the rationale for the change.

Create a sense of urgency: Living requires predictability—too many surprises understandably are frustrating, maddening even. Just consider what we would do if we couldn't count on others to drive on the right side of a street or thoroughfare. Big changes remove predictability.

Only when we fail to get something we want or expect do we reflect: Why did this happen? More important: What can I do to not let it happen again? Fear, loss, and embarrassment can create urgency.

As parents, for instance, it only takes a few public tantrums of our three-year-old before we go into deep reflection. The urgency is palpable. New strategies are tried almost immediately with varying effects. Serious, second order change in an organization requires a similar sense of urgency among the vast majority of its members.

In working with underperforming schools, we find most educators privately have a strong sense of urgency for change, but do not perceive that urgency among their colleagues. How could this be? In most instances, the lack of any discussion among educators leads teachers to assume that few share their high level of concern. Sometimes commiserating rituals suppress the awareness that others are quite concerned. Sharing a sense of urgency opens the opportunity for second order changes. Without a collective sense of urgency, the motivation and energy to make substantial changes will not materialize.

Creating a sense of urgency requires that assumptions and perceptions be set aside and hard core evidence be allowed to speak. First, it should speak to the quality of student learning and the aspirations teachers have for their students. Second, data should speak to the relative gap between students' future needs and what their school currently provides. Fear of sanctions (such as replacing staff) or the promise of rewards (such as cash incentives) will have an effect, but the most compelling sense of urgency arises out of one's professional commitment to support our young—their future or dreams.

If the goal is not compelling to the teachers, the goal becomes more of the same and the reaction of staff will be equally bland and lethargic. A common vision can help teachers visualize the future they want to create, but until they feel that sense of urgency, it will remain words on paper. In fact, Kotter (1996) found that lacking a high sense of urgency "is fatal because transformations always fail to achieve their objectives when complacency levels are high" (p. 4).

Get the vision and strategy right: Nothing is older news in school life than "the vision thing." Nothing is less understood than "the vision thing." As de Brabandere (2005) argues, "We can't do without it, if we are to achieve any major objectives" (p. 63). A vision should connect to our day-to-day decisions, our passions, and reflect a shared commitment in terms or conditions one can observe. For a vision to achieve those goals, a vision statement must be short and easy to remember.

Highly successful organizations establish a link between "why change?" with their vision of what's important. If the link cannot be made between the organization's priorities (the vision) and the changes proposed, then it's a change destined to distract and frustrate people and consume time better used in other ways.

A vision without a plan, though, is just daydreaming. A strategy is a concrete plan for realizing the vision. It is difficult and even dangerous to identify every step in the plan before even beginning to move forward. Most change specialists find that a 300-page strategic plan seldom, if ever, proves useful (Kotter, 1996; Reeves, 2008). Instead, organizations begin with one page, summarizing the intervening goals that allow the vision to become reality. More details will emerge as teams identify the multiple causes of the challenges a school faces and propose intermediate goals and objectives.

Getting the strategy right is perhaps the most challenging task educators face. Working within their circle of influence, teams integrate the vision and goals with the relevant evidence: What's the link between our school's culture and climate and our vision? How can families help realize the vision? What professional development is needed? What are the steps each team should take to get there?

As the strategy for achieving a vision takes shape, it is common for a guiding coalition to discover that one person's proposed solution is another person's problem. It may take some time and struggle for a guiding coalition to emerge from a collection of staff members with different roles and interests. Addressing those challenges is a requisite step for successful change.

Secure buy-in: We can better appreciate the need for a guiding coalition as well as buy-in if we recall some of the earlier efforts to change instructional practice or organization. In the 1990s, school improvement efforts often relied upon a coalition of the willing: A few people who wanted to do something differently volunteered to experiment with changes in practice that should improve student engagement and learning. The naïve assumption was that all those who did not volunteer would watch adoringly and eventually adopt the new practices—and voilà, the innovations would naturally spread throughout the school. Not so. Instead, a coalition of the willing more often became an isolated group that created friction and division among staff. Why do they get those resources? Why do they get all the good students? It's risky to rely on a coalition of the willing to spread innovative practices.

Gaining buy-in begins when members of the guiding coalition acquire a commonality of purpose and commit to a shared vision for the future. The process of achieving the shared purpose and vision includes consultations within departments and action teams, as well as within more informal networks. For buy-in to spread across the school community, the vision has to be perceived by educators as worthy of their time and effort. Without this clear sense of purpose and commitment, the effort will fail. In some instances, the diversity of interests and lack of prior relations may require that either a team or an entire school take time to establish trust—in particular, understanding or even acquiring the shared vision they have for the future. Figure 4.1 illustrates how school staff at one school developed their overview linking needs, teams, activities, and expected outcomes.

Buy-in should begin as one formulates the vision and strategy. One should get as many people involved in thinking about where they want the organization to be in five years and what problems they will need to solve, or practices they will need to change. With that broad base of people involved in establishing the vision, the time needed to secure buy-in is much less than when only a few key leaders are involved. That said, even with

Figure 4.1 Systems Leadership: Developing a Strategy for Change

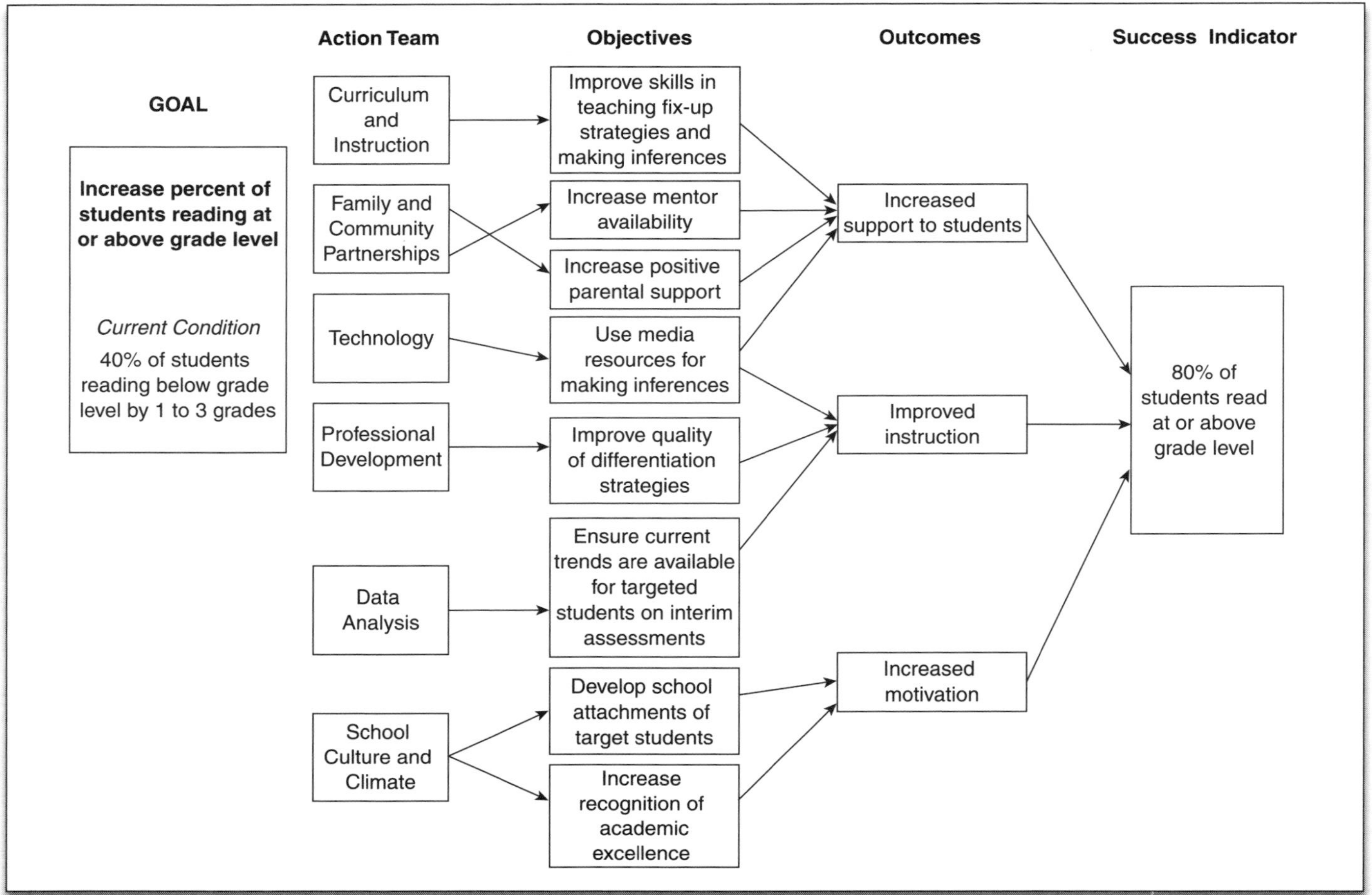

GOAL	Action Team	Objectives	Outcomes	Success Indicator
Increase percent of students reading at or above grade level	Curriculum and Instruction	Improve skills in teaching fix-up strategies and making inferences	Increased support to students	80% of students read at or above grade level
Current Condition 40% of students reading below grade level by 1 to 3 grades	Family and Community Partnerships	Increase mentor availability		
		Increase positive parental support		
	Technology	Use media resources for making inferences	Improved instruction	
	Professional Development	Improve quality of differentiation strategies		
		Ensure current trends are available for targeted students on interim assessments		
	Data Analysis		Increased motivation	
	School Culture and Climate	Develop school attachments of target students		
		Increase recognition of academic excellence		

51

the collaborative effort, the challenge remains to continue to communicate the commitments.

Kotter (1996) insists that one of the reasons organizations fail in their efforts to change practice is that they undercommunicate the vision by 10 to 100 times. Find ways to remind colleagues of the vision. Communicate its meaning, its relationship to everyday actions and the potential it holds for the school and school community. Some organizations place their vision statement everywhere, even on the doors and walls of restrooms. Staff meetings should begin and end with references to the vision—where the organization wants to be in the future and the connection between what one is doing now and that destination. You know you have buy-in when you see evidence that people have begun using that vision in their day-to-day decisions.

Like people in all types of organizations, the buy-in of educators can vary. In an interview with Kevin Butler (2008), Doug Reeves reports on a survey of educators he completed. Slightly over 15 percent of the teachers confronted with new initiatives reported that they intend to lead it. About 50 percent are ready to follow. About 2 percent will be negative about most anything proposed.

Naysayer Roles

Saboteur—Uses personal attacks to close down discussions

Pessimistic Storyteller—Reminds everyone of past failures or lost opportunities

Keeper of the Nightmare—Focuses on the dreams that went awry

Negaholic—Finds something negative about every new idea

Prima Donna—Wants all the best for him- or herself

Space Cadet—Has no idea what's going on

Martyr—Expects others to see the enormous burden of any contribution he or she makes

Deadwood—Along for the recognition

Adapted from Deal & Peterson, 1999

Terrence Deal and Kent Peterson (1999), in *Shaping School Culture*, describe the roles usually assumed by the negative 2 percent—including saboteurs, negaholics, and space cadets. What should be done? Not much. While getting a broad base of buy-in is essential, obtaining 100 percent buy-in is seldom realized and not necessary. In fact, Kotter (1996) finds that seeking support from the 2 to 5 percent remaining naysayers can derail the whole process. Hearing criticism and doubts is good; expecting critical persons to offer constructive solutions is imperative; getting distracted by naysayers is dangerous.

Empower staff: In moving from silos to systems, the first level of empowerment occurs when action teams are established and expected to address schoolwide goals. Administrators and the guiding coalition have critical roles in empowering staff. Ensure that everyone is working within the school's circle of influence. As staff members begin to identify obstacles, remove them. Resources they need? Find them. Acknowledge the risks and accept false starts.

Empowering staff requires getting feedback. Action teams are important vehicles, but informal channels are also helpful. The Technology Action Team may be useful in providing online venues where students or teachers can provide anonymous insights or suggestions.

High-performing organizations—those continually and successfully adapting to emerging needs—create an open environment where not only frustrations can surface (rather than just simmering inside us), but also where colleagues can support each other through the rough spots. Just knowing that others have the same problems can create patience and shared laughter can reduce anxieties. Researchers find predictable patterns of individual frustration and exhilaration during the process of changing practice. Staff members should feel free to express frustrations, and colleagues will often have a solution.

Get short-term wins: Although meaningful change should be for the long haul, experiencing some early successes is essential. A concrete, narrowly focused objective allows for short-term wins such as increasing student attendance, reducing cafeteria chaos, or coordinating afterschool remedial activities with interim assessment results. Even if the goal is subject specific, a large proportion of staff members should have meaningful roles in its realization. If the focus happens to be a particular skill in mathematics, staff should identify and plan for ways in which all parts of the school—music and visual arts, science, social studies, and even cafeteria experiences—can have an impact on the goal.

Action teams allow schools to create a number of ways in which different parts of the school community can have an impact: What activities can parents create at home to give yet another context for understanding, say, proportionality? School Culture and Climate Action Teams may seek to improve class attendance or establish academic awards with a special emphasis on math. The Data Analysis and Technology Action Teams can help with interim assessments. The Curriculum and Instruction Action Team can help all teachers understand the common misconceptions about fractions that they might uncover and address.

Whatever the goal, reach it and celebrate. Celebrate not only the accomplishment of students, but also the contributions of educators.

Essential Roles For Improving Practice

Cheerleader—Finds and celebrates small wins

Coordinator—Fits goals and tasks into larger picture

Coach—Helps others develop new skills

Detective—Always looks for the evidence

Doer—Gets it done

Facilitator—Finds new ways to solve old problems

Helper—Supports colleagues' efforts

Shepherd—Brings wandering sheep back to the fold

Therapist—Reduces frustrations

Consolidate and expand gains: After the first win, reflection is in order: What difficulties were encountered? What needs to change to overcome them? Do policies need changing? Attitudes? Do some roles and responsibilities need to be shifted? What informal roles for supporting school improvement need nurturing?

Perhaps most important, action teams evaluate structures, policies, and formal and informal roles to see how well they support the new practice. Identify the needed changes and incorporate them in the next wave of improvement.

Subsequent waves of reform may focus on generic issues in instruction, such as strategies for uncovering misconceptions. Teachers might work not only within their subject, but also across subjects, to implement strategies that help students confront their misconceptions. Whatever the focus, staff should be reinvigorated with new projects, themes, and change agents.

Make it stick—It's just the way we do business: New practices and processes must become routine. Institutionalize the search for other improvements. Develop and share expertise within and across formal organizational units, and require hard evidence to define problems and determine success.

As action team members learn more about their team's work, they also become experts within their professional learning community, department, or grade-level team. They not only help their colleagues to understand the rationale for, say, proposed changes in an advisory system, but also to troubleshoot problems in adopting new practices or technologies. Making it stick means making it routine. Nothing becomes routine without expert support.

CONCLUSION

Achieving better outcomes for students creates professional satisfaction for teachers. When the changes needed require a shift in the norms, beliefs, or common assumptions of members of the organization, a guiding coalition must provide the evidence that a change is necessary and help create a sense of urgency among colleagues. Second order changes in school practice require a strong and shared vision, a sense of urgency, and a workable strategy. Action teams and the guiding coalition collaborate to develop a strategy for achieving the vision. A school achieves buy-in of all staff by linking current activities with the long-term goal or vision. Action teams help empower staff to realize their goals; leaders identify and celebrate short-term wins, and everyone seeks ways to consolidate the gains and make new practices stick.

CHAPTER FIVE

Barriers and
Pitfalls

The success you will have in reframing the professional life in your school depends, in part, on how you address the existing barriers and deal with common pitfalls that emerge as you begin changes in practice. Barriers to improving practices refer to existing beliefs, norms, and routines shared by the school community that can compromise any effort to improve practice. Pitfalls are common—even predictable—problems that emerge during a change in practices and can lead to lower levels of commitment. Being able to assign a name and definition to a problem is often the first step to eliminating it. This, then, is the modest expectation of this chapter.

In the first section of this chapter, we review the common cultural barriers to improving practice: Low Trust, Blame Bonding, School Legends, and Just Tell Me. The second section focuses on pitfalls that school staff may encounter when trying to solve problems or introduce changes in practice.

BARRIERS

Low Trust: One of the biggest barriers to improving school life or student learning is lack of trust among adults in the school community. It could be between parents and teachers, parents and principal, teachers and principal, or among teachers. Tony Bryk and Barbara Schneider (2002) sought to understand why some public schools in Chicago showed much greater gains in student learning in the 1990s. Schools with the greatest achievement gains in their five-year study were those that developed strong relational trust among members of the adult community.

Bryk and Schneider note that every school day involves a complex web of interdependencies—the quality of classroom instruction depends on whether the bus driver is able to keep to the schedule, whether the school cafeteria provides appetizing and healthy food (try working with cranky, hungry students), whether principals and other administrators are able to calm some angry parents, or whether the right rooms and materials are available.

Teachers may argue that they can close the door and do just fine, but the fact of the matter is that their excellence depends on others—perhaps even more than professionals in many other organizations. It is that vulnerability that makes trust so essential. If one can count on others to "do their jobs" (as parents, principals, maintenance engineers, students, etc.), then one can invest in focusing time and efforts on strategies for effective learning. This is the lubricant needed for professionals to take risks in adopting new instructional strategies or new ways of engaging parents.

Another dimension of trust resides in the degree to which adults demonstrate respect for the craft and skill of others in the community. Every day, everyone, everywhere, necessarily interprets the intentions of others. When we have a history of working with a person, we anticipate reactions or assertions—and that anticipation triggers certain responses in us. The dynamics differ when we have trusting relations: If our trust is robust, we listen before reacting, giving others the benefit of the doubt if what they say is confusing or perhaps even upsetting. When professional respect is weak, we jump to conclusions about the intentions of others. It is this dimension of trust that affects the ability of school communities to engage in public problem solving.

Are some trust relations more important to improving the quality of student learning? While all adult relationships in the school community are important, Bryk and Schneider (2002) find trusting relationships among teachers within a school are the strongest predictors of teacher innovation. Trust relations between parents and teachers are almost as powerful.

Trusting relationships between administrators and teachers are quite important in predicting a school's successful efforts at school improvement, but the essential role for administrators appears to be fostering trust among all the other groups—students, parents, and teachers. A principal working with us noted that he considered his most important responsibility to be "delivering students to classrooms ready to learn." When asked for further explanation, he provided this story: A student was having difficulty with one of her teachers. In a conference with the principal, the student complained that the teacher was gruff and strict. Nodding, the principal said he could see how the student might interpret the teacher's behavior that way, but, in fact, Ms. Horridbegone cared immensely about her students and their learning the process of scientific investigations. The teacher's concern, the principal suggested, sometimes led to her gruffness. In offering this alternative interpretation, the principal created the opportunity for the student to look at the situation differently and perhaps trust that the teacher had her best interests in mind. And thus, she can enter the classroom with a mindset more ready to learn.

Action teams also build trust, especially in large schools where professional interactions have been limited. As team members evaluate various options—be it in scheduling, discipline policies, or uses of technology—the dilemmas that colleagues face as individuals or as professionals are unveiled. On other occasions, it is the unanticipated wisdom, compassion, or creativeness of an educator that nurtures respect and regard from colleagues.

While the issue of trust is, in some ways, inclusive of nearly all the barriers we discuss here, it is important to identify a few specific habits that compromise trust and professionalism. We think three deserve particular attention: Blame Bonding, School Legends, and Just Tell Me.

Blame Bonding: Blame Bonding refers to those instances where teacher collegiality rests upon shared commiseration. Teachers in some schools are great friends with each other; they get along and help each other. It's a tight community of support. At first blush, one might conclude that they have the requisite trust needed to improve the quality of schooling. The collegiality in this instance, though, depends upon rituals that blame others. With Blame Bonding, shared laughter or professional exchanges nearly always include "us versus them" stories. A "them" for the occasion may be low-achieving students, lazy parents, or inept school administrators.

Blame Bonding may make each day go a little easier or foster a little laughter, but it also reduces educators' commitment to improving instruction. The implicit norm is that not much can be done to change their circumstances. After all, the barriers to improvement are someone else's problem. While the problem of Blame Bonding is easy to identify, it is difficult to change.

Overcoming Blame Bonding takes different routes depending on the underlying meaning of the exchanges. One type of Blame Bonding skews toward humor and persists out of habit. We all seek humor to relieve tensions and can inadvertently develop habits that rely on the failing of others. Habits emerge, though, that can create tension—even if was just "all in fun." Teachers seeking relief in this way are no different than soldiers or physicians who rely upon dark humor to push a trauma aside. Yet, the consequences can be different for educators, where vulnerable children and adolescents may be affected. It rests with colleagues in these usually informal settings to help reconstruct the dignity of whoever was the target of the joke—students, principal, or other colleagues.

In the second, more insidious case of Blame Bonding, the accusations lack humor; instead, there is anger. When educators indignantly enumerate the inadequacies of "them," they implicitly opt out of considering solutions. Inevitably, teachers' complaints deteriorate into feelings of despair at the hopelessness of the situation. Typically, what happens is that those who disagree with the blaming statements tend to withdraw and avoid the places frequented by groups of negative-minded peers. It often shows up in comments such as, "I never go to the teachers' lounge." With a little probing, the teacher will claim, "It's just so negative." This leads to further isolation of those who might have a different opinion, inadvertently reinforcing the blamers' belief that everyone agrees with them.

Pulling out of this quagmire requires educators to identify openly the factors they believe are working against all their efforts. A group can identify what they are actually doing that counteracts those forces. A group can re-evaluate the significance of these negative factors by identifying which of those forces have the greatest impact on student learning and, among those, which are within their circle of influence. Resolving this second form of Blame Bonding is best addressed with a professional facilitator who can remain objective while walking the group through a process to analyze the situation and determine how to deal with it.

School Legends: All organizations have legends that orient and inspire their members. Legends that tell of student heroism or educators' sacrifices convey the moral underpinnings of a community. Storytellers embellish actual historical events to add humor, suspense, or more heroic scenarios. Terry Deal and Kent Peterson (1999) find such legends to be benchmarks that define the culture of a school.

In one elementary school where we worked, stories of the principal's career were an integral part of the informal induction of teachers. "She could teach a rock to read," experienced teachers said of her. New arrivals quickly absorbed the meaning that this principal knew her stuff and would expect teachers to develop similar skills. New teachers heard tales of her running down the middle of the street in her high heels—pursuing a young truant she noticed while glancing out her office window. She returned with student at her side. Teachers at the school understood that this principal expected them to *do something.* Don't just complain. Take action.

Reports of her interactions with parents communicated the commitment she had to their children: Once, as the story goes, a parent failed to show up for a conference. Lacking a working phone number on file, the principal drove to the family's apartment complex. The absent mom opened the door and confessed to the principal that she had overslept. The conference was held one hour later. Parents, by personal experience or through the stories of others, understood that this principal took parent partnerships seriously. Thus, the power of positive legends ensues.

Other school legends, though, operate more like the famous urban legends of the Internet—those myths, hoaxes, and folklore that circulate through our electronic mail as fact and create misplaced fears and avoidance. Unlike such legends in school communities, these stories of fear and doom circulating the Internet can be verified with fact-checking websites. No, poison glue is not on our envelopes.

Unfortunately, in the absence of fact checkers, fear-inducing myths and legends circulate in our schools with few corrective forces. During our work with an urban middle school struggling to serve its students, we discovered that teacher collaboration was held hostage by a strike that had occurred 15 years earlier. It was a particularly nasty and protracted strike that had, coincidentally, split the faculty in this school. Every time the faculty encountered even a hint of controversy, the legends surrounding the historical split surfaced and shut down communication. In this unfortunate case, only when one faction of the faculty chose to move to another school did these paralyzing legends receive their proper burial.

When schools have the same recurring disagreements or challenges, a group discussion can surface several things. Sometimes we learn that *most* teachers do not actually buy into the negative legends or debilitating beliefs. In other instances, the discussion reveals that the faulty legend is, in fact, a logo for some strongly held beliefs about learning, human nature, or perhaps adult-child relationships. Surfacing and investigating the validity of the stories can begin with a commitment to a common vision and purpose by the staff. When teachers have the opportunity to talk openly about their vision for the students and the school, the underlying differences become less important. Focusing on their shared purpose and their own efficacy can minimize the relevance of divisive legends. The collective efficacy of the teachers in a school is usually a better predictor of student success than the socioeconomic status of the students (Goddard, Hoy, & Hoy, 2004). When teachers believe they can have an impact, they do.

Just Tell Me: Teachers pride themselves on working cooperatively with district and school leaders—even if they do grumble in the background. The most common phrase we've heard over the years: "Just tell me what to do, and I'll do it." And teachers will!

"Just tell me what to do, and I'll do it" implies a set of procedures or a checklist. Yet, meaningful improvements rarely, if ever, occur when just following a set of procedures. Jeffrey Pfeffer and Robert Sutton's (2000) research on how companies turn knowledge into action confirms that the problem likely begins with those in charge. Toyota executives report that visiting CEOs seeking to learn about the high performance of Toyota plants inevitably limit their questions to the rules

Life With Urban Legends on the Internet

I must send my thanks to whoever sent me the one about poison in the glue on envelopes because I now have to use a wet towel with every envelope that needs sealing.

I no longer have any savings because I gave it to a sick girl (Penny Brown) who is about to die in the hospital for the 1,387,258th time.

I no longer have any money at all, but that will change once I receive the $15,000 that Bill Gates/Microsoft and AOL are sending me for participating in their special e-mail program.

I no longer worry about my soul because I have 363,214 angels looking out for me, and St. Theresa's novena has granted my every wish.

I no longer use cancer-causing deodorants even though I smell like a water buffalo on a hot day.

Thanks to you, I have learned that my prayers only get answered if I forward an e-mail to seven of my friends and make a wish within five minutes.

Because of your concern, I no longer drink Coke products because they can remove toilet stains.

I no longer use plastic wrap in the microwave because it causes cancer.

And thanks for letting me know I can't boil a cup of water in the microwave anymore because it will blow up in my face, disfiguring me for life.

I no longer go to shopping malls because someone will drug me with a perfume sample and rob me.

And thanks to your great advice, I can't ever pick up five dollars in the parking lot because it probably was placed there by a molester waiting underneath my car to grab my leg.

I can no longer drive my car because I can't buy gas from certain gas companies.

If you don't send this e-mail to at least 144,000 people in the next 70 minutes, a large dove with diarrhea will land on your head at 5:00 this afternoon and the fleas from 12 camels will infest your back, causing you to grow a hairy hump. I know this will occur because it actually happened to a friend of my next-door neighbor's ex-mother-in-law's second husband's cousin's beautician . . .

Anonymous Internet Story

and procedures they should adopt. The attempted replications of Toyota's high performance seldom succeed because executives lack an understanding of the overall vision that drives Toyota's procedures.

This problem arises in schools when teachers are given procedural instructions for opening class, managing activities, and so forth, with no real understanding of why they are doing it. Without an understanding of why procedures are what they are, not only will the intended outcomes be missing, but the ability to adapt to different student needs will be impossible.

A second reason for avoiding Just Tell Me appears in the work of Frederick Hess and Thomas Gift (2009). Noted researchers in school reform, they find that school changes that make a difference occur in places where at least 75 percent of the staff have made recommendations for improving the quality of work at their school. Similar to the Japanese auto companies that transitioned smoothly to a new partnership, the expertise of many provided more workable solutions and greater understanding of the change that needed to take place for all (Ouchi, 1983).

COMMON PITFALLS

While barriers are those preexisting aspects of a school's culture, pitfalls are problems that emerge as change is underway. Problems can reduce the commitment of team members. Table 5.1 identifies some common problems that can become pitfalls. Usually, revisiting the core concepts—staying within one's circle of influence, keeping actions and activities closely linked to goals and objectives, and clarifying the roles of team members—will resolve them.

Asking a group of professionals to meet, discuss a problem, and provide a workable solution appears simple. However, anyone who has been a member of a group—church, community, business, or school—knows it is complex. Leaders first must understand the processes needed to unify the team and plan the initial organizational stages. Without thinking through the purpose of teams, the role they will play, and the support they will need, an administrator will be disappointed with team-based strategies for improvement.

One principal returned from a three-day state leadership academy inspired by the stories he had heard from other principals about the teams that were providing advice and developing useful strategies for school improvement. Having considerable confidence in his teachers' abilities, he devoted the next staff meeting to organizing teams around the big problems that were facing the school. Teachers were allowed to volunteer for their particular interest. He asked them to meet and make recommendations at the next month's staff meeting. His disappointment began the next day when he was flooded with questions about what the recommendations should look like, how much time they should spend on the effort, who would carry out the recommendations, and what to do about people who don't want to participate.

After two frustrating months, the principal concluded that "teams just don't work at this school." He had a "good idea" but lacked the understanding and preparation to make it a success: laying the necessary groundwork, anticipating his faculty's concerns, and securing the appropriate support. Most problematic, he had failed to determine how their recommendations would really fit into the school's future. Mistakes such as these can make it more difficult to initiate teams in the future. His failure, though, started with the first step: The principal began the process lacking the first crucial component for any initiative—the data.

A principal and guiding coalition must allow the data to identify a compelling and worthy overarching purpose for the development of the teams. This underlies the entire process.

Sometimes teams or leaders cherry-pick the easy parts of a school improvement effort. The returns are meager. Similarly, schools can establish interest groups, total quality managment–lite, that allow staff to meet in small groups and talk about problems. These are often without the real support of school or district administrators, without the data to inform their definition of the problem, or without learning as the focus of the talk. The results also will be meager. Other times, leaders get distracted by a checklist and forget to reinforce the bigger picture.

In this section, we organize our discussion around symptoms of looming pitfalls. We identify likely causes that include lacking focus or coherence, frustrated or confused team members, team leaders reticent to serve, teachers not fully engaged, poor decisions, and few results.

Table 5.1 Common Pitfalls in Team Development

Symptoms	Causes
A. Lack of focus, alignment, or coherence	1. Team doesn't see how this fits in the big picture or their role in it 2. Too many competing initiatives 3. Poorly planned meetings 4. Lack of data

B. Confusion and frustration among team members	1. Lack of clarity about
	  • Why are we doing this?
	  • What are we supposed to do?
	  • Who is on the team and what are their ideas?
	  • The goals?
	2. Lack of regular communication
	3. Unclear about what others are doing to contribute to this goal

C. Teachers are uncomfortable in leadership roles	1. Team norms not well established 2. School culture rewards and reinforces conformity 3. Team members don't want to appear "special" or "better" than others
D. Disinterest in the task and lack of full engagement	1. Team doesn't see connection to their "world" or priorities 2. Team assigned tasks seemingly unrelated to goals and responsibilities 3. Working on easy vs. powerful items 4. Team members don't think it will make a difference 5. Fear of losing control, fear of time it might take to do something new 6. History of failed, half-baked programs 7. Poorly run meetings
E. Poor decisions	1. Failure to seek out or listen to diverse opinions 2. One person in the group dominates 3. Absence of decision-making criteria 4. Team members avoid differences of opinion or conflict
F. Lack of results	1. Unclear or insufficient data from which to assess gains 2. Failure to set specific objectives and timelines 3. Focus on written reports and planning papers rather than action 4. Failure to use public recording of meetings 5. Lack of accountability to group members

Lack of focus, alignment, or coherence: With so much happening in any one school, it is easy for something new to be seen as "just one more thing to do." Reframing professional life provides an opportunity to bring focus to a school's activities. As described in Chapter 3, successful teams align individual members by addressing the same goal in a committed, systematic, and organized way. Action teams' goals should advance the school's goals. When people, actions, policies and systems are aligned, coherence will create great payoffs and less wasted energy. Synergy develops so that one action begins to propel the others toward the goal (Senge, 1990).

Team members can lose focus when confronted with too many competing initiatives or expectations. The guiding coalition can help determine priorities in the face of too many expectations. If duplication exists, one activity can be eliminated or the two can be combined. Occasionally, committees outlive their original purpose, and these need to be disbanded. Some school goals require more time than anticipated. Perhaps relying more on electronic messages for announcements can create more time to plan or evaluate. Rethinking how time is used can relieve the pressure.

Finally, a loss of focus arises from simple problems, such as poorly planned or poorly run meetings. What are we trying to accomplish today? How does this fit into the big picture? What data do we need to assess our progress? Are team norms being followed? Beginning each meeting by relating the agenda items to the larger goals and ending each meeting by reviewing how actions and plans of the meeting advance the goals related to the larger vision renews focus. The guiding coalition may also post a chart in the teachers' workroom, such as Figure 4.1 in Chapter 4, illustrating how the work of each action team fits together to accomplish the goals. Staff

Achieving a Common Purpose

Between team meetings, current activities of each action team should be on display in a common area. One school had a colorful display in the teachers' workroom. All teachers used the room at least weekly to make copies, so it was easy for everyone to see what all the teams were doing. It was motivating to know that everyone else was working toward the same results.

members at one middle school placed copies of all action team activities in the front of their team notebooks to remind them that they were part of something that would make a difference.

Confusion and frustration among team members: Confusion and lack of clarity about what is to be done and why it is important is a common problem of beginning teams. Comments such as, "Whose idea was this anyway?" indicate that people need to revisit the data or the compelling reasons for this effort. Yes, they've been told already, but sometimes discussions get team members confused. Perhaps they were jotting their grocery list or failed to understand the information and its significance the first time around.

John Kotter's (1996) insistence that one must overcommunicate goals or visions for them to take hold and drive change applies in this case. Reviewing the data at team meetings, posting charts, and displaying the vision in a prominent place in the school will help. We all need reminders to cut through all the competing demands for our time and attention. So, when you hear, "What *is* it that we are supposed to be doing?" you should never consider it a waste of time to repeat the information. Repetition works. Involvement works. Graphics work. Use what you know works.

Regular, frequent, well-organized action team meetings also help people clarify the purpose and their role in it. The norms, guidelines, and processes should be established in the initial training for the members of the guiding coalition and action teams. Sometimes team leaders try to minimize the number or length of meetings. They forget that if meetings are well run, they provide an important opportunity to build relationships, clarify objectives and assignments, make critical adjustments to plans, and hold each other accountable. Regular meetings of the guiding coalition help communicate and coordinate the action teams and thus avoid stagnation or duplication of effort. Revisiting what was learned in the initial professional development for the leaders is, periodically, a valid use of time. The guiding coalition should never limit meetings to just listening to accomplishments and concerns from action teams, but be active problem solvers of behalf of the teams.

Occasionally, the strategy the team chooses to achieve the goal is too vague or too overwhelming. It's similar to the seventh grader who chose to do a semester report on "the religions of the world." Breaking the goal and its related actions into smaller steps that are attainable allows the team to achieve and celebrate the small wins along the way.

Teachers are uncomfortable in leadership roles: A principal expressed surprise when one of his brightest teachers was having a problem leading her action team. After observing the team meetings and debriefing with her, the principal could see that she lacked her usual self confidence. When asked, the teacher confirmed that she was uncomfortable as a leader of her peers. She felt that being the "leader" implied that she was "better" than others. Even more problematic, with more experienced teachers on her team, she felt inadequate.

This situation illustrates why it is so important to establish, upfront for everyone, that team leaders are chosen to be facilitators, not experts and not "the boss" of the team. When team leaders understand their role as a *facilitator* of meetings—making certain that all voices are heard, helping members assess options using evidence, and managing conflicts in ways that help uncover untested assumptions—then confidence can return. Role clarity is key here.

Sometimes, reluctant team leaders benefit from having a cochair who complements his or her skills and can plan cooperatively. It also can reduce potential cynicism that is sure to surface whenever a new way of doing business is introduced into the school.

Another common reason for reluctance is that everyone knows and fears being the target of those predictably negative and resistant colleagues. Facilitators play an especially important role in teams comprised of historically negative people. Without strong facilitators, the negative members can dominate the discussion. A timekeeper can help everyone to have an opportunity to participate. Establishing a norm at the first meeting that expects "no blaming, no complaining" provides the ground rules that a facilitator can use to redirect the discussion.

Disinterest in the task and lack of full engagement: Disinterest in teamwork arises most frequently when a disconnect exists between the assigned tasks and team members' sense of urgency. Both action teams and the guiding coalition should review proposed initiatives with this issue in mind.

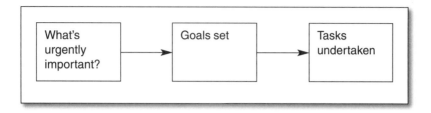

Are the tasks clearly related to the goals? Have people become buried in the details and forgotten where they are headed? Have team members lost sight of the goal?

Disinterest also arises when administrators give assignments to teams with no apparent connection to school goals or an action team's expertise or responsibility. Sometimes principals have an urgent need for research on a topic or support for planning an event. While it is certainly acceptable to make such assignments, both the assignment and the activities need to connect with the larger responsibilities of the team and the school goals.

Disinterest emerges easily in schools with a history of great ideas that turn to dust only months after the inspiring speaker presented them. Under the circumstances, the team will benefit from evaluating how, in fact, this effort can be different.

Sometimes teams get bored. They've chosen an easy goal that minimizes effort but also minimizes any potential impact. When the task they've chosen isn't sufficiently meaningful to make it interesting to them, they lose interest. One can avoid this problem in the planning stage by considering: What will be the payoff if we choose to pursue this activity? Does the payoff justify the effort? Will it really move the school closer to its goal? It reminds us that the goal isn't just to "do something," it is to do something that is significant enough to make a difference. When a difference can be made, most of us are interested and engaged.

Investigating schools that have made a difference against seemingly impossible odds stimulates interest and commitment. Reading about, visiting with, or talking to other schools generates new ideas and inspiration. Each school, however, must translate the basic principles into their own situation for them to be successful. No one-size-fits-all solution exists.

Some seemingly disinterested people are actually afraid; they fear that they will not be good at a new way of doing something or fear having to learn some new system when they have one that already works perfectly well for them. Sometimes our desire for perfection inhibits our willingness to change. Change brings the risk of goofing up, often publicly. Learning takes time and effort. Facilitators can surface and minimize fear by helping team members talk about what changes in practice would be required by a proposed change, what benefits it may bring, and a reality check on the learning needed to successfully implement the change.

Poor decisions: Just because a group of people makes a decision doesn't mean it will be a good one. As we discussed in Chapter 2, poor decisions most often arise when we fail to draw out the expertise, wisdom, and perspectives of all members in the group. In those instances, a few team members often dominate the discussion and others lose interest.

Most teams benefit from establishing what would constitute a good decision. For example, one team established that a good decision:

- is based on data,
- is legal,
- is consistent with board policies,
- is good for students,
- is reasonable with the available or accessible resources required,
- will be supported by parents and community,
- will help toward achieving the school goal, and
- will be supported (not undermined) by members of the team.

Action teams should adopt decision-making criteria at the beginning of their work. Often, team members cannot anticipate the value of the criteria in advance of problems. They find themselves in an intractable debate lacking the criteria or standards to resolve it. Other times, teams do establish criteria, but they prove to be inadequate for the dilemma that the team confronts. Whatever the case, it is necessary to commit as a group to criteria that help define a good decision. They should provide an impartial and systematic way to evaluate options.

Establishing decision-making criteria minimizes conflict. Lacking agreement on the criteria for evaluating options, conflicts emerge as team members rely upon different criteria. Most people avoid conflict, so they will clam up and withdraw at the hint of spirited disagreement. As part of the group norms, each group should address how they will listen to each other and how they prefer to handle conflict. Just as with decision-making criteria, it will save time and produce better relationships and more productivity.

Lack of results: All of the pitfall symptoms listed in Table 5.1 can lead to the final one: lack of results. But, lack of results sometimes comes from failure to determine how the results will be measured from the very beginning. Groups often determine a focus, do the research, organize for action, and implement the plan without considering how they will measure the impact of what they have accomplished. How one will measure impact or success should always be part of the planning process. We need criteria not only to evaluate "Did we do it?" but also "What difference did it make?" with explicit measures of the goal. Achieving worthwhile goals provides energy and confidence to address new challenges. The guiding coalition and Data Analysis Action Team play important roles in avoiding mishaps.

Some teams get stuck in the procedural aspects of teams— holding meetings regularly, filling out the meeting forms completely, reporting to the staff about what they are working on—but never get to the action and achieve results. They are busy but not productive. Every group becomes more accountable with some type of public display that shows the preaction data and postaction data. Depending on the action team's focus, the data will vary, but it can be a way to help shape the groups' thinking and hold them publicly accountable to achieving results. The likelihood of realizing goals increases greatly when all action teams' efforts address the same school goal.

CONCLUSION

Barriers are preexisting conditions in an organization that can undermine meaningful change. Every organization—hospitals, manufacturers, police departments, or schools—has barriers.

Discovering what barriers exist, identifying their underlying causes, and working to resolve them are the first steps. That said, it is seldom necessary or beneficial to consider public confessionals as part of overcoming barriers. Rather, finding appropriate ways to renew one's professional vision and building trust and respect among adults through collaborative efforts will allow schools to overcome such barriers.

Pitfalls are conditions that emerge during the effort to change practices that compromise an organization's ability to reach its goals. Many pitfalls can be avoided or minimized by doing the required work upfront to establish and prepare the leaders and teachers to be full participants in the teams that will effect improvement. However, pitfalls of some types are inevitable. So, when they do occur, they should be addressed as learning opportunities and considered just a normal part of the cycle in developing strong teams.

Section II

Each chapter in this second section focuses on one of the six core issues usually addressed by an action team. Each provides a brief overview of the research that can inform the choice of objectives and activities as well as guidance on the initial steps action teams should take to get started.

Both the guiding coalition and action teams need persons to assume three roles: chair, timekeeper, and recorder. We suggest having cochairs, especially at the action team level. Having cochairs helps to ensure continuity of meetings when one of the cochairs is absent, provides two people to help plan meetings, and spreads the responsibility of leadership more broadly across the school. The action team chair is responsible for developing the agenda of each meeting, presenting proposals and planning documents to the guiding coalition, monitoring the progress of activities, and ensuring that the team takes time to celebrate accomplishments—big and small.

The timekeeper is responsible for ensuring that agenda items are addressed within the time allotted for them, giving a heads-up to fellow team members when they need to bring closure to one topic and move to another. At the beginning of the meeting, members assign the amount of time they need to devote to each topic. The timekeeper helps team members keep track of time, but as issues emerge, the team may choose to alter the plan by reducing the amount of time devoted to other topics or arranging for an additional meeting. Sometimes the chair chooses to perform the role of timekeeper.

The recorder develops a written record of a meeting, including any new responsibilities assumed by members of the team and makes certain that all team members receive a copy of the record within a week of a meeting.

When teams first get started, they usually find it necessary to meet biweekly. As things begin to move, the meetings may be limited to once a month, with some activity occurring outside of meetings.

Below, we provide additional details on the ways the guiding coalition and action teams should be formed, the responsibilities of both, how a guiding coalition interfaces with action teams, how one should assign members to an action team, and the steps all action teams take in getting started.

THE GUIDING COALITION

A principal should make the initial selection of the members of the school's guiding coalition following the general principles outlined in Chapter 2: varied experience and expertise, leaders from various parts of the organization as well as informal networks of teachers. The principal selects a chairperson for the guiding coalition. The chairperson is responsible for developing the agenda for each meeting in consultation with the principal and assigning the roles of recorder and timekeeper for each meeting. An agenda should be available to coalition members a week prior to their meetings.

Establishing a shared goal for all action teams: Gaining leverage requires that all action teams direct their efforts toward the same goal. Using assessment, attendance, and climate data, the guiding coalition recommends a common goal. For example, if reading performance is consistently weak, the guiding coalition may wish to review subscale scores to see if there is a particular area that is critically problematic for all grade levels. Sometimes the issue is not evident on a subscale, but related to reading particular types of documents, such as technical versus fiction. The goal may focus on an issue that is undermining student learning, such as high absentee rates among students. High-performing schools may see that their needs are not in a specific subject area, but rather in the low performance of one or more subgroups. Goals may have that level of specificity as long as the team can anticipate how each action team can contribute to that goal.

Determining indicators of success: The guiding coalition establishes the indicators that will be used to monitor schoolwide progress. Trend level data is important in establishing a target, as are comparisons with district and state data. Previous rates of progress on interim assessments are especially useful. Selecting subscale performance indicators will increase the likelihood of realizing an improvement.

Over the long term, the Data Analysis Action Team will support the guiding coalition in securing data for determining goals and monitoring progress—making certain that charts or graphs are available to both analyze problems and establish indicators of success. If the data team has yet to be formed prior to the initial meeting of the guiding coalition, the principal should recruit a few staff members likely to become members of the Data Analysis Action Team to assist in collecting or preparing the data. The initial meeting of the guiding coalition is largely a waste of time without such data.

Coordinating and monitoring action teamwork: The guiding coalition is responsible for ensuring that each action team's objectives focus on the shared goal, complement the work of other teams, and progress in a timely manner. Oftentimes, action teams encounter road blocks that may require some adjustments to their strategy, and the guiding coalition serves as a resource in resolving those problems.

Members of the guiding coalition hold a unique position in the life of a school. They, along with the principal, have an understanding of how various activities fit together, how they collectively address an important goal, and how they link to the larger vision the school has for its future. As such, they must be advocates for the future and help their colleagues continue to see the big picture.

Action teams propose year-long objectives aligned with the general goal, and the guiding coalition should be prepared to review them quickly and simultaneously. A prompt review is critical; action team momentum is lost when the team waits too long to begin planning. Looking at the proposals simultaneously allows the guiding coalition to look for synergy and points of collaboration for each.

The guiding coalition should review proposed objectives with these considerations and questions in mind:

1. *Evidence:* Research supports the link between the proposed objective and the school goal.

2. *Alignment:* Taken collectively, do action team objectives complement each other and lack redundancy?

3. *Leverage:* Is the expected impact worth the effort involved?

4. *Coordination:* Should other action teams be involved?

After the proposals are approved, each action team develops an activity plan to reach its objective. Again, the guiding coalition reviews them. The plans should be reviewed with the following considerations:

1. Are planned activities clearly linked to the objective?

2. Are there any missing action steps?

3. Is timeline compatible with other events in the school?

4. Are recommended team collaborations appropriate and specific?

Occasionally, as a school undergoes a radical transformation, either through difficulties in its own performance or through changes in policies or expectations, a guiding coalition may need to assist with reformulating a school's vision or help consider what types of changes educators should expect with the pending changes. Action teams should be an integral part of assessing what changes will need to be made and how best to implement them. Oftentimes educators have no control or input over *what* will happen, but they do have control over *how* it will happen.

The guiding coalition's cycle of activities should follow that of school improvement planning. Over the long term, the cycle begins at the end of the school year: after receiving annual assessment data, the guiding coalition reviews accomplishments and identifies a new or revised goal that will guide the future work of action teams. The other major markers in the cycle of activities include a mid-course review of action team work and then, at the end of the year, a time for reflecting on accomplishments, assessing, and celebrating the effectiveness of the school's effort.

ACTION TEAMS

Membership

Making good use of systems thinking requires that administrators devote careful attention to the composition of each action team. This is the only nonnegotiable. If one is careless with the composition, reframing the organization will be just a nice idea whose potential will not be realized.

Teams should be formed on the basis of

- teacher preferences for action team;
- representation of all subjects and special areas;
- diverse thinking styles; and
- diversity of experience, ethnicity, and gender.

Teacher preferences for action team: Staff should be working on issues of interest to them. Ask each staff member to identify—in rank order—the three team issues they would like to address. Inform people in advance that every effort will be made to put them on a team of their choosing, but all of the factors mentioned previously will be used to develop the teams. Rarely does everyone become a member of the action team that is their first choice. However, each staff member is usually able to serve on one of his or her top three choices. Staff need to know in advance that they may not get their first choice.

If for some reason it is not possible for a person to become a member of one of his or her three choices, a principal should talk with the person individually and explain the situation. Sometimes a staff person has a special skill or leadership ability that leads a principal to assign that person to a team he or she did not choose. Publishing a team membership list without explanation for either of these situations can create misunderstandings that are difficult to resolve.

While it is important for teachers to have some choice, the effectiveness of each action team hinges on the diversity of its members. Teams achieve their maximum impact when they are diverse and representative of all parts of the school.

Representation of all subjects and special areas: To ensure that needed information is readily available to action teams and that timely communication flows throughout the system, each action team must be comprised of members representing all sectors of the system. Each grade, content area, the arts, special education, guidance, and administration should be represented on each action team.

Diverse thinking styles: Groups with the best problem-solving capacity have members with diverse thinking and problem solving styles. The Myers-Briggs Type Indicator (MBTI) and the Kiersey Temperament Sorter provide good indicators of an individual's preferred approach to solving problems. Individuals may complete the online questionnaire inventory without charge. Provide staff with an explanation of the meaning of their resulting "type," how it will be used in the formation of action teams, how it improves the quality of solutions, and how it is used for developing highly functioning groups.

Diversity of experience, ethnicity, and gender: These also add to the richness of the problem-solving process and should be taken into consideration when establishing the teams.

Assigning Team Members

Considerable time and frustration can be eliminated by making an individual index card, or, preferably, a Post-it Note, for each staff member. It should include the staff member's name, team preferences, grade level, subject area, and temperament type. If you have a relatively small staff, you may make one large chart with action teams listed as the columns and subject area (if this is a middle or high school) or grade level (if this is an elementary school) as rows. If you have a large staff, it is best to create a chart for each action team, using subject area as the columns and temperament type as the rows.

Building each team requires an iterative process:

1. Begin by giving every staff member his or her first preference—place each Post-It Note in the appropriate position on the chart.

2. Make adjustments for subject area (or in elementary schools, for grade level). Which teams lack representation from which areas? Begin working with second preferences to redistribute memberships, ensuring that all areas are represented on each team.

3. Check to see the balance of the MBTI or Kiersey temperaments represented in each action team. Fill the missing temperaments by making adjustments among staff who chose that action team as a second choice, then third.

4. Review teams for balance. In addition to ensuring that all teams have members from all subject areas and grade levels, administrators should ensure a diversity in experience, gender, and ethnicity.

Action Team Responsibilities

All action teams share responsibility for the following:

1. Working toward a common goal of improving students' learning and well-being through collaboration and shared leadership.

2. Becoming "experts" in the action team's topic area by
   - collecting and sharing information and data about current conditions in the action team's area, and
   - suggesting improvements within the action team's area that are based on an understanding of the needs of students and staff, well-developed theory, current literature and research, and other appropriate sources of best practice.

3. Ensuring that interdependencies among team efforts are taken into account by
   - understanding the roles and responsibilities of other teams;
   - taking advantage of opportunities for shared work with other action teams that is coordinated to avoid redundancy

and looking for synergistic approaches leading to working smarter, not harder; and

- recommending actions to the guiding coalition for coordination and review to ensure feasibility and likelihood of advancing school goals.

4. Communicating goals, objectives, and accomplishments to the entire school community.

5. Developing and executing plans and quickly sharing problems as they emerge with the guiding coalition.

Specific action team responsibilities include the following:

School culture and climate: Focuses on aspects of a school's culture most likely to undermine the quality of education available to students: health, safety, belonging, and esteem of students, faculty, and staff of a school.

Data analysis: Supports the guiding coalition and action teams in securing and analyzing existing data, helps the coalition and action teams collect new data relevant to their goals and objectives, and develops expertise in accessing data that can support professional learning communities.

Family and community partnerships: Helps identify and support effective ways for parents to support student learning and students' capacity for self-discipline, for schools to help parents build their own networks, and for educators to use parent volunteers effectively. The team also helps the school find ways to use community organizations and businesses to support school goals.

Curriculum and instruction: Works on ways for cross-discipline coordination or collaboration to improve student learning by increasing the modalities and contexts in which students gain a better understanding of concepts or more fluency with important skills.

Professional development: Identifies district and state workshops or online courses that are aligned with school goals, supports the development of professional learning communities within the school, ensures that an induction program is available for teachers new to the school, and assesses the impact of school-based professional learning and likely needs for the future.

Technology: Helps staff improve their productivity and practice related to school goals with existing technology, helps improve use of tools that support teaching and learning, ensures that staff have support system for solving simple operational problems, and provides recommendations for long-term technology acquisition.

Getting Started With Action Team Work

The initial meeting of an action team should include the following:

- Develop norms and assign roles
- Agree on criteria for good decisions
- Establish regular meeting times
- Review the essential processes needed from Chapter 3
- Review the school goal and relevant data
- Review the school improvement plan
- Read and discuss the action team background information
- Profile school's strengths and challenges in their area
- Identify changes that address school goals
- Propose a general objective for the team

If each of the above activities is completed at the initial meeting, teams will have strategies in place to evaluate conflicting or competing proposals, enable future meetings to run smoothly, and develop a shared understanding of the issues in their area of work.

With each team addressing these points, the entire staff are grounded and headed in the same direction. They are poised to address their action teams' role in achieving the school's goal. With the foundation of data, a common goal, and a link to the school improvement plan, the teams will have more focus, create alignment, and possess the ability to have an impact.

Without this common beginning, the teams will choose projects or activities in which they may have an interest, but that may not eventually converge and impact the students and the school community. Skipping a step does not become evident right away, but if you review the barriers and pitfalls in Chapter 5, you will notice that often the cause of future problems is the omission or incompleteness of one or more of these steps. It is better to take it step by step. Occasionally, even after following all of these steps, it is still desirable or necessary to revisit them to reinforce their importance and relevance to the team's work.

The initial proposal: The previous steps lay the groundwork for the team to make an initial proposal for an area of focus using the form shown in Table II.A. Developing a proposal allows the guiding coalition to approve a general direction *before* a team invests time in developing detailed plans.

First, the guiding coalition verifies the link between the proposed objective and the school goal. Second, the guiding coalition reviews the proposals for complementarity. Third, the guiding coalition looks for connections between the action teams—places where the teams might work collaboratively. And last, administrative approval is needed to make sure the proposal is consistent with district policies. Most often it is best to develop and submit two proposed objectives in the event one is not appropriate or timely.

This process is somewhat different than most people experienced in previous groups. In the past, individuals or groups had an idea, ran it past the principal, and then moved forward. Or, a group was given the mandate "to do something" about an issue, so they developed a plan and moved forward. Acting in isolation was part of the problem. The "old way" is not systemic, but rather can create chaos at worst or have little lasting impact at best.

When the proposal is approved by the guiding coalition, then the team can work out the details and timelines necessary for moving forward. The approval step causes a slight delay at the start, but less frustration in the long run. Explaining this process clearly prior to developing the proposal minimizes the confusion between the proposal format, its purpose, and the action planning stage.

Table II.A   Action Team Proposal Form

School _____

Action Team _____ Date _____

1st Option

Proposed objective: _____

_____

Research evidence on efficacy of objective: _____

_____

Link with school goal: _____

_____

Data supporting need for objective: _____

_____

Support needed from:

Other Action Teams:

☐ Curriculum & Instruction   ☐ Professional   ☐ Data Analysis
                             Development

☐ School Culture &   ☐ Family & Community   ☐ Technology
   Climate   Partnerships

- -

2nd Option

Proposed objective: _____

_____

Research evidence on efficacy of objective: _____

_____

Link with school goal: _____

_____

Data supporting need for objective: _____

_____

Support needed from:

Other Action Teams:

☐ Curriculum & Instruction   ☐ Professional   ☐ Data Analysis
                             Development

☐ School Culture &   ☐ Family & Community   ☐ Technology
   Climate   Partnerships

- -

Members present:

Developing an Action Team Plan

A plan requires detailed action steps, timelines, and individuals assigned to be responsible for each step. The chair should expect everyone on the team to have a responsibility in some phase of the plan. Table II.B provides guidance in developing this plan.

Sequencing: Some actions depend on the completion of other tasks. They should be noted as sequential and the tasks on which they depend identified. One will need to check carefully to see that the proposed dates work. For instance, if Jason agrees to get names and addresses of the executive directors of local community organizations and Ophelia agrees to print and mail the letters, Jason will need to complete his task before Ophelia can accomplish hers.

Coordinating: The team chair should meet with leaders of those teams with whom they need to coordinate and identify specific responsibilities that other action teams will assume. These other activities should be outlined with timelines specified.

The planning form actually becomes a valuable record for making expectations clear and keeping track of activities from one meeting to the next. After the action team's plan is approved, e-mailing it to team members is a helpful way for them to keep track of their responsibilities and timelines.

Implementation, Monitoring and Adjusting, Celebrating

As plans become actions, unanticipated barriers or glitches emerge. The guiding coalition keeps track of the progress of each team and helps them adjust their plans to remove the problems they may have encountered. Celebrating accomplishments should be integrated thoughout the year as teams achieve milestones or simply overcome an unanticipated problem. Before each new year, a time for reflection on accomplishments and lessons learned builds the capacity of all teams to work more effectively in coming years.

Table II.B Action Team Planning Form

Action Team: _____ Date: _____ Objective: _____

Research supporting link between planned activities and objective: _____

_____

_____

Success indicators: _____

Steps	Person(s) Responsible	Due Date	*Sequence?

Plan of Work

*Note: Does this step require sequencing? What steps must be completed before this one can begin?

Collaboration agreements with
other action teams:

☐ Curriculum & Instruction ☐ School Culture & Climate
☐ Professional Development ☐ Family & Community Partnerships
☐ Data Analysis ☐ Technology

Members Present:

CHAPTER SIX

School Culture and Climate

S chool culture refers to the shared beliefs and assumptions that guide the individual decisions of members in a school community. As observers or members, a school's culture is visible through what Terrence Deal and Kent Peterson (1999) call the "living logos"—those actions and words that serve as "placards, posters, and banners" (p. 65) for the beliefs and values educators hold. This includes beliefs about what and who are important, what students must understand to have a fulfilling adult life, and what good parents do. In culturally diverse communities, unfortunately, people often hear different things from the same signal.

Educators signal what schooling is all about with more than their words. How classroom time is used, the types of exams and assignments given, and interactions with students outside the classroom convey the value educators place on student learning. Administrators signal their priorities by their interest in protecting time for learning, what's displayed in the entry halls of their schools and on a school's website, the availability of textbooks and classroom supplies, what's discussed at faculty meetings, and what they celebrate with teachers and students.

School climate, if we dare to make too big a distinction, refers to the behavioral responses of students and staff to the cultural signals they see and hear in a school. Researchers find that a positive school culture is most likely to exist where norms and signals make students feel respected and safe, where the rules are clear and fairly enforced, and where students are integrated and attached to the life of the school. Student misconduct arises when one or more of these conditions are absent.

The work of the School Culture and Climate Action Team revolves around the health, safety, belonging, and esteem of faculty, staff, and students—aspects of school culture that are most likely to undermine student learning, directly or indirectly. Given that schools differ substantially in the cultural challenges they face, some parts of this chapter—and, yes, even the mission of the action team—necessarily will vary greatly across schools. In this chapter, we provide some baseline indicators for school climate, discuss the fundamental issues related to school safety, and explore how schools develop student and teacher attachments to school in ways that promote not only a healthy culture, but also a commitment to teaching and learning.

SCHOOL CLIMATE INDICATORS

Table 6.1 provides a list of commonly used indicators of school climate. The School Culture and Climate Action Team should profile its school and compare with other comparable schools or the district data. Reviewing multiple years of data will provide a more reliable profile than one year only. With those baseline indicators in mind and their school's goal, the action team can begin to formulate which areas of school climate may need most attention.

Teacher and student absenteeism serve as baseline indicators of the quality of a school's culture. For teachers, job satisfaction and involvement in school life are predictors of absenteeism. The U.S. Bureau of Labor Statistics (2008) estimates that on any given school day, 5.3 percent of the nation's teaching force are absent—a comparison not so favorable with the absenteeism of the entire U.S. labor force, which is 3.3 percent. Researchers (Miller, Murnane, & Willet, 2007) estimate that the effects on student achievement begin when a teacher's absence rate exceeds 10 days.

Not surprisingly, national estimates for student absenteeism are difficult to find. In low-performing high schools, the daily attendance rate of students hovers between 60 and 75 percent. Daily

Table 6.1   School Climate Indicators

- Absenteeism rates of teachers and students
- Theft records
- Reported incidents of bullying
- Rates of in- and out-of-school suspensions
- Frequency of classroom disruptions
- Adequacy of texts and classroom supplies

attendance in high-performing high schools ranges between 90 and 95 percent. One cannot attribute poor attendance of either teachers or students to any single cause. Year-to-year changes often have reasonable explanations such as bad weather or flu epidemics. That said, looking over multiple year trends does tell a story. Some portion of absences in any occupational sector occurs simply because people just don't want to be there. Thus, absentee rates are valuable indicators of the health of a school's culture.

Many national school indicators point to satisfied parents and well-meaning students in our public schools today. According to national surveys (Council of Urban Boards of Education, 2008), 84 percent of parents of urban school children are happy with the school their child attends and trust the teachers with whom their child is working. A recent survey, sponsored by the Council of Urban Boards of Education (2005) and administered in 108 schools in 15 districts of varying size, found that most students feel safe at school, do not experience bullying, feel that teachers respect students, and are optimistic about the future.

A national study, cosponsored by the U.S. Department of Justice and the National Center for Education Statistics (NCES), also provides encouraging news: Between 2003 and 2008, the proportion of students reporting they had been physically bullied declined from 23 to less than 15 percent. Principals reporting frequent verbal abuse of teachers declined from 13 to 9 percent between 2000 and 2006 (National Incidence Study of Child Abuse and Neglect, 2009). Most educators would agree: We cannot be content when 15 percent of principals report bullying incidents as fairly routine events, nor when any schools report frequent verbal abuse of teachers. In both instances, the effects of such incidents reverberate to students who were not victims.

National data suggest that while students in most schools feel safe, students attending large, urban middle schools have different experiences from others. Middle school principals at schools with high rates of transferred students or high teacher-to-student ratios report bullying problems more frequently than any other type of school—over 50 percent report that bullying occurs at least once a week or daily (NCES, 2006).

Undoubtedly, bullying ranks high on the list of safety concerns. Statistics and perceptions of the extent of bullying vary, though. Thirty-two percent of students ages 12 to 18 reported being bullied in 2007 (Dinkes, Kemp, & Baum, 2009). The vast majority (79 percent) report occurrences inside school and 17 percent of those bullied report occurrences once or twice a week, or every day. A reporter for the *Charlotte Observer* in Charlotte, North Carolina begins an article on bullying with this claim: "Students and administrators might as well be living on different planets. Students across the state say it is common for bullies to taunt and hit them or their classmates, and teachers do little to stop it. Superintendents and principals say bullying is a small problem and policies to discourage it work well" (Bonner, Klahre, & Chavez, 2009, par. 1).

After the School Culture and Climate Action Team profiles its school climate with statistical data, members may wish to dig deeper with observations. Table 6.2 lists some of the school signals that provide further expression of a school's climate. Depending on the school's statistical profile, the action team may wish to make some systematic observations of one or more of these signals.

Table 6.2   Observing Climate in Schools

- Adults monitoring hallways
- Teachers routinely sharing resources
- Students and teachers interacting outside of class
- Students avoiding certain areas of building
- Cleanliness of building and grounds
- Displays of student work
- Persistent signals of high expectations for students' futures
- Diverse opportunities for student recognition

SCHOOL SAFETY

Regardless of the statistics, the question remains: What makes something a big or small problem? The frequency with which it occurs? The number of students affected? Whether or not someone was injured? Daniel Goleman (2006) finds that there is little difference between a school culture that allows students to be ostracized and one that allows students to inflict physical pain on others; both impair the cognitive ability of students in ways that can account for a decline in learning.

Researchers also find that years later, long after the bullying has stopped, adults who were bullied as youths have higher levels of depression and poorer self-esteem than other adults. Those who bully others as adolescents commit crimes that lead to incarceration at much higher rates than the average population.

Bullying is most likely to occur in places and at times that lack adult supervision. Like most other discipline problems, it is more likely to occur where students and adults are indifferent to the behavior or when enforcement of rules is erratic. Bullying occurs at much higher rates in middle schools than either high schools or elementary schools.

According to Olweus, Limber, and Mihalic (1999), relying on strategies that focus on individual bullies seldom work. Instead, a schoolwide commitment is required. Schools should raise awareness of bullying, form clear rules and norms, and recruit every adult in the school (including janitors, cafeteria workers, even crossing guards) to supervise the spaces where bullying could occur. Olweus and colleagues suggest that students be asked to make pledges that they will not bully others, that they help those who are bullied, and find ways to include those students who appear to have few friends. While a minority of students in any particular school experience bullying, leaving it "unchecked" affects the sense of safety of many students.

Encouraging students to protect victims can reduce the incidence of bullying behavior. Educators can cultivate a school culture that fosters students' sense of responsibility for protecting peers as well as one that cultivates respect for diverse cultures both within and outside the school community.

We begin by looking at those conditions in a school that are most likely to affect the safety of students and, yes, all staff: the physical environment, routines and procedures, and perceived fairness in enforcing rules.

The physical environment: A school's building and grounds are the first "logos" seen by students, staff, and visitors. Their physical appearance is the first signal to students and teachers about the likelihood of whether they will feel respected and safe once they get inside. For students and visitors with less honorable motives, it's a sign that this is a place where misbehavior and crime may be invisible, or even tolerated. It's no surprise that turnaround principals make the physical appearance of a building the first order of business.

People behave differently when buildings look neglected versus well kept. Urban sociologists George Wilson and James Kelling (1982) coined the term *broken windows* to explain the rate of crime in a neighborhood: Compared to neighborhoods where eyesores are promptly eradicated, neighborhood crime is more likely to occur when broken windows are not replaced quickly, trash is accumulating in vacant lots, or perhaps abandoned cars can be found on streets. Their argument is that criminals view broken-window neighborhoods as much safer places to commit crimes because they are less likely to get caught and residents are less likely to feel comfortable reporting crimes. Cleaning up neighborhoods has thus become a central weapon against crime throughout the United States.

Stephen Plank, Catherine Bradshaw, and Hollie Young (2009) thought it would be useful to evaluate the degree to which the theory of broken windows had any application to schools. They studied 33 middle schools over a three-year period and found that when school buildings were neglected (trash on floors, broken chairs, or dirty bathrooms), marginal students more likely misbehaved, and good students lost confidence in the educators' ability to provide a safe environment. Clean and well-maintained school buildings, then, are a necessary, but not sufficient, condition to establish a safe and orderly environment for students and adults.

> **School Community Signals**
>
> A school in the southern United States has a huge, colorful quilt that greets visitors. The first graduating class of a then-new education program created the quilt, each student working with teachers and parents to add a personal patch describing the connection of the school to its community.

School routines and procedures: School routines and procedures affect students' sense of safety—some increase it, others diminish it. School routines for such things as movement between classes, lunchroom activities, boarding buses, and so forth provide an environment that is protective for most students.

After the tragic incident at Columbine High School, local school boards and educators aggressively worked to acquire the necessary equipment and policies to reduce safety risks. Camera equipment in hallways, security checkpoints, chained doors, and even armed district police forces are increasingly common in today's schools. Yet, the most recent statistics from the U.S. Department of Justice finds that the rate of violent crimes at schools is higher than the rate experienced away from school (Dinkes, Kemp, & Baum, 2009). While one may consider it a statistical anomaly, the shift in safety at schools relative to elsewhere in students' lives has been moving in that direction for almost a decade.

Zero-tolerance laws that sought to ensure a safe school community continue to produce incidents that make little sense. In 2009, a rowdy lunchroom food fight in a Chicago middle school resulted in 25 arrests. That same year, an overly exuberant new Cub Scout brought his new Scout cooking utensil—with fork, knife, and spoon—to school without his parents' knowledge. The zero-tolerance law required a 45-day suspension and attendance at a reform school for 45 days. Fortunately, as his mother home schooled him, the local school board quickly made adjustments in their zero-tolerance policy for first graders. Not surprisingly, many American citizens wonder if some punishments have grown out of proportion to the misbehavior.

While the issue of the proportionality of punishment to the "crime" captures most critics' attention, another—unanticipated—consequence must be kept in mind: normalizing of misbehavior. More is not always better. When suspension rates are high, a school runs the risk of normalizing deviance—increasing the likelihood that students will view the punishment as "just part of school life." When many of their peers are in a similar predicament, it can even be fun. While research has not identified the point at which the incidence of disciplinary action comes to normalize the experience, we feel confident that any rate above 20 percent of the students receiving out-of-school suspensions risks changing the meaning of the incident from negative to positive.

Normalizing Deviance?

It was a brisk fall day when I drove down a four-lane country road on my way to work. I noticed that a "DUI crew" was picking up litter along the side of the road. In Tennessee, convicted DUI drivers often are required to don orange jackets with "DUI Worker" emblazoned on the back and pick up litter alongside major thoroughfares. While I had yet to develop an opinion on the value of this practice, I certainly acquired one that morning.

Ordinarily, such stigmatized folks walked alone with their bodies slumped to suggest some type of embarrassment. But not this group, not this morning. They walked together, laughing and chatting and only occasionally stuffing litter into their giant plastic trash bags.

As I got closer, I realized that these were all young people, both young men and women, and they were having a jolly good time. Hearing what they were saying didn't seem necessary. I could only imagine that before the morning was over, they'd made arrangements to meet at some watering hole that week. Whether that was the case or not, it was clear that they failed to view their situation with any embarrassment. Clearly, they had not only normalized their deviance but found it a good opportunity to meet like-minded youth.

S. B. Kilgore

Johanna Wald and Lisa Thurau (2010) argue that the use of restorative justice is much more effective and appropriate than arrests or out-of-school suspensions. Restorative justice refers to the practice of requiring misbehaving students to perform services that make amends to the people they have hurt or inconvenienced. In the case of food fights, Wald and Thurau suggest that requiring students to clean the cafeteria for a month is not only more appropriate, but also ensures time for peers to reflect on the consequences of the misbehavior.

Classroom procedures affect the likelihood of student misbehavior—as every new teacher knows. National records show that most discipline problems occur in class (Skiba, Michael, Nardo, & Peterson, 2002). Most often, students are sent out of classes for defiance or disruption (Gregory & Weinstein, 2008). Clear procedures, expectations, and consequences are the foundation for good student behavior.

Initial assessments of why students become defiant, though, suggest that something more than good procedures and routines may be needed. Researchers find that teachers who rely on relational management prevent misbehavior problems. Students will trust teachers—and therefore willingly seek to comply with rules or fulfill expectations—when they sense a personal interest in their well-being and success. Anne Gregory (2008) and others refer to it as a "relational approach" to gaining student cooperation. Signaling a personal interest in students begins by knowing something about their interests and concerns and following up occasionally to find out more about them.

Relational Management Approach

- Teachers know students' names and take time to chat with them outside the classroom.
- Teachers know something about students in classes and check in with them about recent events in their lives (e.g., new brother, sports victory).
- Teachers convey confidence in a student's future.
- Teachers show concern when students are absent.

Classroom grouping routines can also generate disruptive behavior—especially with adolescents. As Daniel Goleman (2006) notes: "The social universe of school is at the center of teenagers' lives" (p. 306). Good instruction inevitably involves teamwork among students, but when teachers allow students to choose with whom they'd like to work, the results reduce the sense of acceptance among a majority of the students in the classroom. While various procedures can be used to avoid that outcome, Elliot Aronson (2000) advocates "jigsaw classrooms" where students from divergent social groups work together to master an assignment. His strategy follows a basic principle in social psychology: When people from groups that ordinarily hold hostility toward each other work together with a common goal, they come to like and respect each other. If group assignments reinforce cliques, however, not only does the social order suffer, but so, too, does learning (Goleman, 2006).

Rules are clear and fairly enforced: Students attending school in high-poverty neighborhoods are especially sensitive to the degree to which adults create a safe environment. Absent such, students' need to act tough is real. Wayne Walsh (2000) notes:

> Conventional values may be a liability in large urban school districts. In the absence of strong support for good behavior and effective discipline for bad behavior, students will lower their risk of victimization by means of their own invention. Unfortunately, the defensive strategies they adopt may only fuel a vicious circle. (p. 100)

High-poverty urban schools do vary considerably in the rates of misconduct among students, leading one to conclude that educators can have a substantial effect on student misconduct regardless of the neighborhood environment. Walsh (2000) finds, in his study of middle schools in Philadelphia, three strong predictors of school disorder: students' perception of the clarity of rules, fairness of rules, and respect for students. Among students at urban schools participating in the Students as Allies project (What Kids Can Do, 2004), only 38 percent thought administrators "enforced the school rules evenly." How schools address such a problem will vary. But no solution will be effective until administrators have a deeper understanding of students' perceptions: Do they think "high status" or "the good kids" get away with misbehaving in ways that others don't? Do they perceive an ethnic bias? Or do they perceive a surveillance issue: Are administrators absent from the places where students misbehave?

Teachers have an important, but seemingly incidental, role in signaling concern for respectful behavior. Teachers cannot afford to ignore the slight insults embedded in student chatter—be it in their classrooms or the hallway. Just pretending that one doesn't hear rude adolescent conversations defines a school's culture for students in negative ways. After the School Culture and Climate Action Team has had an opportunity to review basic indicators of the school's culture, members may wish to observe school interactions to gain a better understanding of certain climate problems that could manifest themselves in the school.

CREATING ATTACHMENTS TO SCHOOL AND COMMITMENTS TO LEARNING

Gary Wehlage and Robert Rutter's (1986) classic research on student dropouts demonstrates the great need for students to develop strong attachments to school—through peer friendships, recognition, and adults who build their confidence about their future or provide counseling in difficult situations.

For those students with many "odds" against them, it only takes one adult who cares passionately about their future to make the difference. In fact, this is the single best predictor of a student changing those odds. Those attachments can be with a teacher, maintenance staff member, secretary, or administrator. Such relationships not only cultivate attachments to schooling (thus bringing them back each day ready to make appropriate efforts to learn and follow school rules), but they also buffer children against emotional harm and help them acquire social skills that will allow them to have rewarding relationships as adults (Coyl, 2009).

Students who are given responsibilities in school have a stronger attachment to schooling than those lacking them. Some responsibilities may be embedded in extracurricular activities; others may be simple classroom responsibilities—as mentors, greeters, or even trained mediators for peer conflicts or misunderstandings. Some schools seek to energize marginal students in extracurricular activities.

Student recognition can vary substantially across schools. At one extreme, an elementary school may invent awards just to ensure that every fifth grader receives one. At the other extreme, usually a high school, recognition is restricted to football players and cheerleaders. It's not hard to assess the dangers of these extremes. Most often, though, schools may overlook the value of providing recognition for academic accomplishments. Sometimes the best form of recognition is the simplest: expressing confidence in the future students can build for themselves.

An ancient, but classic, study of high schools by Roger Barker and Paul Gump (1964) demonstrates some of the limitations of large schools: the limited opportunities for students to participate in student activities and sports. Regardless of size, high schools have only one football team, one debate club, one student government, and so forth. While each of these can vary in size, schools can become so big that the enrollment begins to impact the likelihood that students could acquire some attachment to school or recognition—increasing the likelihood that an average student might become indifferent to school. The data reviewed earlier (NCES, 2006) suggest that middle school students may be especially challenged in establishing attachments to staff and peers when the enrollment exceeds 800. Middle schools also have fewer avenues for student recognition than high schools, yet their students likely have a greater need for such.

Educators serving a culturally diverse student population must be proactive in developing student awareness of and respect for different cultural values and norms. Even seemingly small differences in eye contact and physical proximity signal different intentions across ethnic cultures. School Culture and Climate Action Teams with a diverse student body may wish to reflect on the degree to which seemingly divergent cultures are honored, not only in assemblies and celebrations, but also in the mundane transactions in classrooms and school offices. Consulting with parents and civic leaders from various cultures may provide the team an opportunity to uncover practices that compromise some students' attachment to the life of the school.

Respect for Diversity: Some Indicators

- Students feel valued and respected by their classmates and teachers.
- School staff understands the norms and values of the various cultures represented in their student population.
- School expectations—norms and procedures—are consistent with diverse community values.
- Students respect the diverse cultural norms of students at the school.
- School staff and students appreciate the commonalities in beliefs and values among the diverse cultural backgrounds.

"Service learning is a promising practice," says Shelley Billing (2010) in a *Principal Leadership* article, "but like other instructional practices, it must be done well to produce positive outcomes" (p. 30). Here are Billing's suggestions:

- Provide quality service while learning important academic objectives.
- Meet a real community need.
- Gather data on the need before and after service.

- Allocate resources and support, which include a coordinator, professional development, time, and transportation.
- Provide visible and tenacious adult support throughout the program (p. 30).

Possible Civic Groups Within a School

- Welcome pals: Students orient new students to building, services, and opportunities at the school.
- Opportunity task force: Student task force identifies resources and services in the community that are available to students at the school.
- School climate advisory group: Students help action team discover the root cause of behavioral problems in school—messy cafeteria, hallway problems, etc.
- Advocacy groups: Student task force targets common health problems and identifies ways in which students can help address them.
- Community or school history team: Students research local history and prepare publication to share with new students and families.
- Peer tutors: Each department or grade level establishes a program for student tutoring.

Students as part of the solution: Students build important attachments to schooling when they can take some responsibility for improving the quality of school life. Early results from Students as Allies (What Kids Can Do, 2004) suggest that students may be a critical vehicle for turning around school performance or simply making a good school better.

With the support of the Students as Allies program, schools in five major urban areas—Chicago, Houston, Oakland, Philadelphia, and St. Louis—launched student-led research on their high schools. In addition to using some core survey items across all schools, students developed questions specifically for their school. Their unique questions varied considerably, with high-performing schools focusing on academic pressure students experienced and other schools focusing on what made classroom work engaging or why students might consider dropping out.

Schools recruited both obvious student leaders and those lacking any such recognition. In Oakland, the students working with

Students as Allies were enrolled in a special leadership class—designed to cultivate nontraditional leaders. One student in the program described the outcome of their efforts:

> I think [it] offers a way for students to change the vibe of the school and how it operates. A lot of times students are scared to stand out and do something different or positive because there is a lot of antagonizing. In Oakland schools, many people don't want to see anything positive; they're satisfied with the status quo and just come to school to kick it and not really learn. (What Kids Can Do, 2004, p. 3)

Building Student Attachments to Schools

- Students have multiple ways in which they can learn about the extracurricular activities available to them.
- Marginal students are encouraged to join extracurricular activities or assume other responsibilities at school.
- Students have multiple opportunities to establish a close relationship with at least one staff member at the school.
- Students from diverse cultures have opportunities to participate in extracurricular activities that are congruent with their values and norms.

Allowing students to help create solutions to school problems—be it the messy cafeteria, bullying of others, or just the "vibes" in the building—not only solves many of the problems, but also cultivates leadership talents that otherwise might have remained dormant. A young participant in the Students as Allies (What Kids Can Do, 2004) project says it well: "You love school when it makes you feel smart. When you know the teachers care about you and your future, when they act like they think you'll be someone in life" (p. 1).

Educators' attachment to their schools: Surveys of teachers' priorities and concerns consistently point to the high value that teachers place on the opportunity to collaborate with their colleagues (Public Agenda and Bill and Melinda Gates Foundation, 2010). While there are many ways in which collaboration can occur, such as professional learning communities and action teams, the time available to do so is still quite limited.

The never-ending waves of new expectations for student learning, new constraints on how and when one teaches what, and yes, the complexity of responding appropriately to student behavioral problems often undermine the quality of the professional life in schools. Grumbling has a certain cathartic function. A bit of grumbling about the state legislature and a few jokes about the school board will relieve tension, but they don't solve the problems educators encounter each day in the classroom.

Peter Senge (1990) and others note that organizations tend to undervalue dialogue—that is, conversations among staff that seek to understand the reasoning or values behind the positions or beliefs they hold. Anthony Bryk and Barbara Schneider's (2002) observations of staff and team meetings in urban schools led them to conclude that faculty meetings usually are limited to courtesy talk; everyone gets to talk, but no one is listening. It's not clear why this pattern exists, but unless dialogue goes beyond any one person's understanding of a situation, it's just ritualistic chatter. The structure of action teams provided here is intended to foster honest and constructive conversations. Professional learning communities also create a foundation for trust and honest dialogue.

Attachments to school will not be strong in the absence of honest dialogue. The interdependencies make all members vulnerable. Principals depend on teachers' support to maintain order as well as respect from their community. Teachers need some type of parental affirmation to be effective with their students. Everyone, then, feels vulnerable, or, to use Senge's (1990) framework: "Often in the guise of being helpful, we shelter someone from criticism, but also shelter ourselves from difficult issues" (p. 250).

Bryk and Schneider (2002) argue that dialogue emerges when there is relational trust among teachers. The level of collegial trust is best seen by the degree to which

- teachers feel respected by other teachers,
- respect among colleagues rests upon their professional expertise and leadership in school improvement projects,
- teachers find it okay to discuss worries and frustrations with their colleagues, and
- teachers sense that their colleagues really care about each other.

Acquiring an attachment to colleagues and the unique mission they share may emerge from faculty traditions. In Amherst, New Hampshire, for example, a large, progressive, and relatively affluent high school created an end-of-year tradition: the "Viking funeral." At the end of the last day of school, staff members share that year's memories. After writing their thoughts down, they walk to the river and place their notes into a cardboard "Viking boat" ready to float with the current. As one faculty member explains:

> The Viking funeral is the place to say goodbye to many things. . . .
> Many of us let go of fear and frustration. . . . Each year some-
> one discards feelings of insecurity, of not being good enough
> or smart enough. . . . We have stated publicly that we were
> releasing anger, pain, rage, and sadness. We have used the
> occasion to mask the silly and the profound. . . . It is our most
> sacred ritual. (Silva & Mackin, 2002, p. 128)

CONCLUSION

In summary, a school's effort to create an environment where students and faculty feel respected and safe involves attention to the physical environment and to the routines and procedures of the school as well as each classroom. Clarity of rules and their fair enforcement is equally important, but apparently more difficult to achieve if one takes the perceptions of students seriously. Creating a positive school climate requires that educators find ways to build students' and educators' attachments to school—both through personal relationships and assuming responsibilities in the civic and extracurricular life of the school.

CHAPTER SEVEN

Data Analysis

"Water, water everywhere, but nary a drop to drink"—the complaint of *The Ancient Mariner* echoes today among educators: data, data everywhere, but nary a drop to inform. How can it be that so much data appears to be of such little use?

A recent report from the U.S. Department of Education (2009) estimates that the proportion of teachers able to access an electronic student data system grew from 48 percent in 2005 to 78 percent in 2007. Even with that striking change, the teachers surveyed report that the data they can access are of minimal use in their instructional decisions.

For teachers to find data useful to instructional decisions that they make in specific classrooms, teachers need either (1) individual student level data within a time span that they can remediate problems or (2) cohort data from the previous students they taught with which they can improve their instructional approach. Yet, only about a third of all teachers can retrieve diagnostic or benchmark data for their current students. Even fewer can access standardized test results for their current or previous students (U.S. Department of Education, 2009).

The problem: The lack of enthusiasm for or confidence in data-informed decision making in schools originates, we think, from the type of data most commonly made available to educators in the past decade: aggregate data for subgroups of students (such as ethnicity, English language learners, and so forth) or for grade levels. Aggregate data—both by virtue of the typical presentation format and the numerous, but subtle, statistical issues involved—create confusion between the relevant and irrelevant. But more important, such data can only inform a small portion of individual teachers' concerns.

Thus, the first confession data advocates need to provide teachers is that aggregate and cohort data cannot address the following daily instructional decisions:

- Which students are struggling in what ways and for how long?
- Which students might be grouped for targeted instruction?
- What activities seem to be working best for which students?

The second confession data advocates must make is that the form in which data are presented often clutters the relevant information with the irrelevant. The cohort and subgroup data shown in Table 7.1 illustrates a worst case scenario. It's an excerpt from the National Educational Technology Trends Study (NETTS) 2006 interview protocol used to assess teachers' facility with complex data. For each grade level, the table reports the number of students at each proficiency level subdivided by gender, and within gender, subdivided by ethnic group membership (U.S. Department of Education, 2009).

Table 7.1 also provides the percent of female and male students within each grade level taking the tests by their ethnic identification. Thus, of the fourth grade females completing the test (i.e., "percent of students tested"), 47 percent were Latina, 26 percent were White, and 24 percent were African American. Exactly how does one propose that teachers use this information?

The table also provides the (now less and less interested) reader with the actual numbers of White, Asian, Latino, and American Indian students in the third, fourth, and fifth grades who scored within various proficiency levels—below basic, basic, and so forth. If one had yet to notice the problem with the number of students in this analysis, the numbers within each cell clearly indicate that it is useless to evaluate the potential differences across gender and ethnicity.

While the data shown in Table 7.1 are immensely useful to those who wish to evaluate the statistical finesse teachers can

Table 7.1 Survey Item From NETTS 2006: Proficiency in Reading Comprehension

Grade	Gender	Ethnicity	Number of Students Tested	Percent of Students Tested	Mean Scale Score	Number of Students at Each Proficiency Level			
						Below Basic	Basic	Proficient	Advanced
3	Female	African American	18	26%	439	5	7	5	1
		Asian/Pac Islander	1	1%	610	0	0	0	1
		Latino	17	24%	428	5	6	5	1
		White	34	49%	449	4	13	11	6
		Total Female	70	100%	444	14	26	21	9
	Male	African American	18	23%	436	6	6	5	1
		Asian/Pac Islander	2	3%	452	0	1	0	1
		Latino	31	40%	430	8	7	14	2
		White	27	35%	448	6	11	7	3
		Total Male	78	100%	438	20	25	26	7

Grade	Gender	Ethnicity	Number of Students Tested	Percent of Students Tested	Mean Scale Score	Number of Students at Each Proficiency Level			
						Below Basic	Basic	Proficient	Advanced
4	Female	African American	18	24%	441	3	8	5	2
		Asian/Pac Islander	2	3%	462	1	0	1	0
		Latino	36	47%	436	8	12	12	4
		White	20	26%	472	2	7	8	3
		Total Female	76	100%	447	14	27	26	9
	Male	African American	16	23%	442	2	8	5	1
		Asian/Pac Islander	0	0%	NA	0	0	0	0
		Latino	29	42%	438	5	12	10	2
		White	24	35%	456	3	13	5	3
		Total Male	69	100%	445	10	33	20	6

(Continued)

Table 7.1 (Continued)

Grade	Gender	Ethnicity	Number of Students Tested	Percent of Students Tested	Mean Scale Score	Number of Students at Each Proficiency Level			
						Below Basic	Basic	Proficient	Advanced
5	Female	African American	19	26%	463	2	6	8	3
		Asian/Pac Islander	1	1%	317	1	0	0	0
		Latino	34	47%	452	4	14	10	6
		White	19	26%	507	1	6	7	5
		Total Female	73	100%	467	8	26	25	14
	Male	African American	17	23%	449	2	6	6	3
		Asian/Pac Islander	3	4%	560	0	0	1	2
		Latino	34	46%	448	7	13	11	3
		White	20	27%	468	3	6	8	3
		Total Male	74	100%	467	12	25	26	11

Source: U.S. Department of Education, 2009, Appendix B.

demonstrate with issues of sampling error and sampling size (which was the original purpose), they also illustrate the type of data that—regardless of an educator's statistical finesse—do little to increase teachers' appreciation of the potential of data to inform their classroom decisions.

The third and final confession to be made is that interpreting aggregated data requires not just an understanding of basic statistical principles, but also experience with identifying how statistical issues manifest themselves in aggregated student performance data. Table 7.2, again from the NETTS 2006 survey instrument, aptly illustrates the potential problem and confusions, as well as the likely conclusion that data can say whatever one wants it to say.

Making sense of Table 7.2 requires that one understand how a distribution of scores affects summary statistics—in this case, the mean mathematics score. A careful observer initially may be startled to observe that while very little difference exists between the mean mathematics scores of Latinos and African Americans on this sixth-grade mathematics assessment, the difference in the percent of students demonstrating proficiency is dramatic. The proportion of Latino students reaching proficiency is much lower than for African Americans. So, is this an instance where one can say things are bad or good, depending on the numbers one reports? Yes, it could be.

Understanding the reason, however, for divergent answers may be small comfort. As a summary statistic, a mean is quite sensitive to extremely high or low scores—especially in small samples (note that there are only 31 Latino students in this school). A few Latino sixth-grade students are performing exceptionally well—perhaps with

Table 7.2 2005–06 Achievement in Grade 6 Mathematics by Ethnicity

Group	Number of Students	Mean Math Score	Percentage Proficient	Number Proficient
African American	228	67.5	61	139
Latino	31	66	48	15

Source: U.S. Department of Education, 2009, Appendix B.

even perfect scores, but most Latino students are performing quite poorly. The high-scoring students "pull up" the mean score, implying equivalence between the performance of Latino and African American students. Unfortunately, while these differences are interesting, they have little substantive value, but rather just reinforce the "whatever" about statistics.

With these problems in mind, the Data Analysis Action Team must, of necessity, assume some responsibility for ensuring that aggregate (or cohort) data made available to educators

- includes the relevant and excludes the irrelevant,
- does not become trivialized by small numbers, and
- relies upon graphs and other easily interpreted representations.

The future: Fortunately, we are on the cusp of dramatic changes in the type and quality of data that will be available to educators. The 2004 reauthorization of the Individuals with Disabilities Education Act expects schools to use interim assessments throughout an academic year to identify students who may need some form of remediation. National and state commitments to relying upon the gains of individual students to assess progress in student learning will allow more educators access to individual student data. Finally, the 2009 American Recovery and Reinvestment Act (ARRA) provides additional funding to states to develop the data systems needed to track individual student progress over time. With each succeeding year, then, more and more teachers should be able to access data for timely remediation of students and to diagnose their own instructional weaknesses.

Currently, though, the type and availability of data differ dramatically across states and, in some cases, districts within states. The role and responsibilities of a Data Analysis Action Team will differ accordingly. In general, the team should serve as a resource to the guiding coalition and other action teams. This team should focus on providing relevant data to

- improve student learning,
- discover root causes of persistent problems, and
- monitor the impact of new initiatives.

In this chapter, we focus on what types of data can answer what types of questions, the types of comparisons that will help educators narrow the possible explanations for problems they encounter, and the kind of evidence that will allow them to assess the validity of their explanations. We cannot, on the other hand, begin to address a variety of other issues that the Data Analysis Action Team may encounter—survey instruments they may wish to use, the statistical issues that may arise in some types of analysis, good presentation formats, and so forth. It is best for teams to rely upon materials associated with the software available to them.

DATA TO HELP IDENTIFY STUDENT LEARNING NEEDS

Providing data that allow educators to identify changes needed to improve student learning requires, as we noted earlier, identifying the relevant data, providing data in easily intelligible formats, and knowing when small numbers will trivialize a discussion of differences. Individual student data and aggregate data can, and do, answer different questions about student learning. We discuss both.

Providing individual student data: Three reasons prompt us to begin with the use of individual student data to improve student learning:

- Federal requirements for schools to have interim assessments for all students
- The ease with which teachers may translate the evidence to remedies in their classrooms
- The small number of statistical issues that emerge from such data

Which students are struggling? Obviously, many teachers easily identify the difficulties of individual students as a routine part of instruction—through the questions they ask or the problems a student can or cannot solve. The opportunity to uncover problems in student learning, though, varies by the amount of time an educator works with a student, the number of students he or she serves, and the technology available to help monitor student learning.

Ideally, then, interim assessment data gathered by district or state data analysts can serve as confirmation of a teacher's assessment. It may, in fact, be somewhat frustrating. ("Yes, I know Roberto is having difficulty with fractions, but I have yet to figure out what will work for him.") Even with for the most astute teacher, however, some student difficulties go unobserved and interim assessments will be helpful.

For individual interim assessment data to be useful in classroom instructional decisions, though, they need to provide at least two data points to establish a point of comparison. With low scores at one data point, for instance, a teacher must consider whether or not a student's poor performance is a result of concepts not understood in previous grades or problems with recent material.

The Data Analysis Action Teams may wish to consider archiving other useful data to assist educators in evaluating the needs of individual students. Portfolios of student work may prove invaluable in helping professional learning communities uncover common misconceptions among their students. Many web-based tools allow educators to look at student work longitudinally. Various applications of Web 2.0, for instance, can archive student portfolios that provide a school-based data base for analyzing student work over time. The Data Analysis Action Team may be able to enrich the opportunities for professional discussions by helping to organize data repositories for student work.

Which students might be grouped for targeted instruction? If student-level data is available and can be easily manipulated, sorting students by grade and subscale performance can be one of the easiest tasks for a Data Analysis Action Team. Grade-level teams or departments may form small group tutorials or—depending on the extent of the problem—incorporate challenging concepts in a variety of contexts outside the subject area where many students appear to be encountering problems.

What instructional approaches work best for which students? It almost goes without saying that neither diagnostic data nor standardized assessments provide many hints about the types of instructional activities that will work best for a student with specific learning needs. Teachers usually rely upon word of mouth to help separate the useful from the useless, but it is possible to build more systematic evidence. Data Analysis Action Teams at large schools may be able to build a "best practice" database for teachers at their school—beginning modestly with types of students in greatest need, for example, English language learners. Perhaps they could begin with data from computer-driven tutorial programs and identify which programs appear most effective for which types of students.

A number of websites such as WeTheTeachers provide educators with informal reviews of teacher-created activities and often include specific information on their success with specific populations of students.

Instructional management systems, with open architectures, that capture the types of assignments given to students with specific learning needs can, over time, be mined for answers to the best approaches—just as cardiologists are able to do at various hospitals.

> **Types of Student Data**
>
> - State assessments
> - Baseline assessments
> - Interim assessments
> - Running records/DIBELS
> - Class grades
> - Extracurricular activities
> - Interventions
> - Attendance records
> - Suspensions
> - Disability status
> - Retention history
> - Writing samples

Caution for using student-level data: In helping colleagues interpret the results of individual diagnostic or summative assessments, the issue of measurement error cannot be ignored; that is, for any given estimate learning gains, there is a certain degree of error. Statisticians provide estimates of the range of that error—usually for any given assessment. When looking at individual student data that is wildly inconsistent with other classroom-based performance data, teachers may need to respond cautiously and look for other evidence to resolve the discrepancy.

Reviewing aggregate data: While we may have some complaints about aggregate student data, it actually provides insight into more general issues that compromise student learning. Aggregate or cohort data can be very useful in discovering problems in curricular alignment, as well as identifying types of students whose diverse needs are not being met with current instructional strategies.

Robust analyses, however, usually require that educators have an accurate inventory of the data that are available. Like the hidden computers in some closets, educators may be surprised to learn what data they can easily access. Knowing what data are available to whom, when, at what level of aggregation, and for which grades and subjects provides an overall understanding of what types of questions can be addressed. How many years of state assessment are available and with what other information? Armed with this information, a Data Analysis Action Team can respond more readily to queries and concerns from other teams. For state assessments, in particular, the Data Analysis Action Team should know the number of years for which data should be considered comparable. For instance, when benchmarks for proficiency shift or new standards are introduced, the year-to-year comparability is lost.

Aggregate data are especially useful with learning problems that persist across multiple years for nearly all students or for a specific subgroup. For instance: Why do our eighth-grade Latino students persistently drop in their mathematics proficiency? Why do our reading comprehension scores appear to be especially weak for all students in the eighth grade? It is not the task of a Data Analysis Action Team to provide the answers, but rather to know what data will be needed to evaluate potential explanations.

To address these types of questions, a good analysis should begin with multiyear comparisons of the grade level, cohort, or subgroup in question. Comparisons should include the following:

- Other subgroups or cohorts in your school
- State versus district performance
- District versus school performance
- Comparable schools in your district

For instance, where subgroups, like Latinos (or girls), differ in their performance from other ethnic groups (or boys), it is more likely the result of the relative effectiveness of instructional strategies for different groups rather than one of alignment between what is taught and assessed. If it were the latter, all subgroups would "suffer." Consider the poor performance of Latinos in eighth-grade mathematics shown in Table 7.3.

Comparison with other subgroups: Looking at the row marked "TOTAL," one sees that in the fifth, sixth, and seventh grades, Latinos were, on average, quite similar to Whites not of Latino origin. However, Latino performance drops noticeably in the eight grade where, on average, they get only 41 of 60 items correct compared to 48 for Whites not of Latino origin. Looking at the subscales, the comparisons of these two groups reveals consistent and meaningful differences for only the algebraic subscale.

Table 7.3 Four-Year Performance in Mathematics: Comparison of Latinos With Whites Not of Latino Origin

GRADE	5th			6th			7th			8th		
		Mean Correct			Mean Correct			Mean Correct			Mean Correct	
Sub-scale	#Items	W	L	#Items	W	L	#Items	W	L	#Items	W	L
Number sense	13	12	11	9	6	7	9	7	7	12	10	10
Measurement	12	8	8	9	7	6	9	7	6	12	10	10
Geometry	13	9	10	9	6	7	9	7	7	12	11	9
Algebraic	9	6	4	8	6	4	9	7	5	12	9	5
Data	12	8	9	9	7	7	8	6	6	12	8	8
TOTAL	59	43	42	44	32	31	44	34	31	60	48	42

Comparison with state and district performance: If eighth-grade Latino performance dips at the state or district level in ways similar to what happens at your school, then something about instruction that is shared with all schools in the state or district should first be considered. If the dip in performance is limited to your school, then something about the instruction that is specific to your school should be considered first.

Reviewing multiple years of data of Latino performance in mathematics, we see that the problem likely began years earlier: algebraic thinking skills were problematic for this group as far back as the fifth grade. It was Latinos' high performance in other subscales and the increasing "weight" of algebraic thinking skills that led the school to detect the problem only at the eighth-grade level.

What if one discovers that the district pattern for Latino performance had been the same as this school's? The problem, then, may reside in the materials shared by all schools. The text may have relied upon illustrations or examples that were not meaningful to Latinos, or the Latino students may have different prior understandings than those assumed by the text. On the other hand, if the Latino performance pattern is unique to this school, then activities specific to the school must be considered.

Learning from other patterns in student performance: Jaime Escalante, the California mathematics teacher whose extraordinary capacity to motivate students was captured in the movie *Stand and Deliver,* encountered a challenge to his work that few teachers survive. Teaching advanced mathematics to high school students in the barrios of Los Angeles, Escalante sought to instill his students with confidence in their ability by having them "sit for" nationally recognized exams. In 1982, all of his advanced mathematics students passed a College Board Advanced Placement exam. The victory almost fell apart, though, when College Board administrators became suspicious of the high rates of success among his students. They were especially curious that all students not only responded incorrectly to an item on the exam, but they all chose the same incorrect answer (also known as "distracters").

As the facts unfolded, though, it was clear that nothing untoward occurred during the administration of the exam, but rather that his students acquired misconceptions from Escalante's instruction—that is, his misconceptions were replicated by his students. Fortunately, the College Board realized the problem was not a case of cheating and honored all of his students' passing grades.

Escalante's challenge, though, is our gain. Item analysis, such as that done by many testing agencies, can be of great use to educators seeking to improve instruction. Two types of instructional issues can be revealed with item analysis: First, of course, is the Escalante error, whereby instructors or texts can provide incorrect analyses or procedures for solving problems and the vast majority of students will select the same incorrect answer. Second, and less appreciated, is evidence of an alignment problem, occurring when the vast majority of students give incorrect responses to one item, but they differ in which incorrect item (or distracter) they choose; it is then likely that the concept was not part of the instructional program. Table 7.4 illustrates these differences.

INVESTIGATING THE ROOT CAUSE OF PROBLEMS

Often, schools encounter problems that require a systematic exploration of more than just changes in curriculum and instruction. Why does the lunch schedule for our fifth graders consistently go awry? Why does student attendance consistently drop in February? Root-cause analysis helps educators solve these puzzling problems.

Root-cause analysis emerged out of a systems approach to understanding organizational problems. Analysts realized that many solutions adopted by organizations only addressed the symptoms of a problem rather than the root cause. Frequently, doctors treat only the symptoms—perhaps it is antibiotics and nasal spray for a persistent sinus infection. Yet, the underlying cause may be the stress the patient is experiencing that compromises the immune system. Unless and until the stress is removed, the patient will likely repeat the symptomatic treatment again and again. Organizations experience similar cycles when they fail to address the root cause of problems.

Analysts rely on several strategies to move beyond symptoms and into root causes. The most common strategies used in the

Table 7.4   The Escalante Error and the Alignment Problem

Escalante Error

	Response to Item				
Student	Correct	Wrong Answer #1	Wrong Answer #2	Wrong Answer #3	Wrong Answer #4
1			X		
2			X		
3			X		
4	X				
5			X		
6			X		
7			X		
8			X		

Alignment Problem

	Response to Item				
Student	Correct	Wrong Answer #1	Wrong Answer #2	Wrong Answer #3	Wrong Answer #4
1	X				
2				X	
3		X			
4					
5			X		X
6		X			
7			X		
8					X

educational context are "the five whys" and fishbone analysis. Regardless of the strategy, data are important to the process: first in helping to describe the problem and second, by providing confirming or disconfirming evidence as explanations surface.

The five whys: The five whys is an open-ended approach that takes the initial answers to a question and digs deeper (iSixSigma, 2002). For each explanation given, a facilitator will ask, "Why is that?" For instance, suppose educators want to address the question of why students are so frequently late to school. An abbreviated version of how the five whys conversation might proceed follows:

1. *First why:* Why are more and more students arriving late to school?

   First answer: Because of the traffic jam outside the entrance.

2. *Next why:* Why is there always a traffic jam outside the main door?

   Second answer: Because too many parents drive their children to school.

3. *Next why:* Why do parents drive their children rather than use school buses?

   Third answer: Because many children are bullied on the buses.

4. *Next why:* Why does the bullying occur?

   Fourth answer: Because of competing cliques of students.

Through this exploration with the five whys (fortunately, only four were needed here), we have moved from the possibility of needing a traffic cop to the possibility of needing bus monitors, or possibly, some work on the cliquish behavior in school. Experienced organizational facilitators find that with five or less whys, solid hunches about the root cause(s) of problems emerge.

Obviously, a productive use of the five whys requires data to anchor the discussion. The Data Analysis Action Team should identify relevant points of comparison that can inform the conversation.

In the tardiness case, the discussion should be preceded by statistics on the incidence of late arrivals over an extended period of time as well as some comparisons by grade level and with nearby schools.

Once the apparent root cause(s) are identified, then data should be collected or evaluated to verify the conclusions. In the example: Are fewer children using the bus services? Are some bus routes more affected than others? Has there been any increase of complaints from parents about the safety of their children?

Fishbone analysis: Fishbone analysis attempts to determine the root cause of problems by systematically reviewing basic factors that could affect the problem. Which basic factors one explores may depend on the question, but for this type of analysis to be effective, a systematic review of all factors should occur. For instance, factors that might explain minor behavioral problems include the environment, the technology or equipment, the methods or procedures in place, or monitoring processes. On the other hand, if the behavioral problems are more serious, perhaps a review of a broader range of issues is in order. Figure 7.1 illustrates using the core factors in school performance, which could be discussed in terms of how they might be contributing to a problem. The core bone identifies each of the factors that should be discussed. The bones extending out on each core represent objective facts about that core issue that may be contributing to the problem.

ASSESSING THE IMPACT OF NEW INITIATIVES, POLICIES, AND PRACTICES

An important responsibility of the Data Analysis Action Team is to help the guiding coalition assess the impact of new initiatives, policies, or practices. In most instances, the new initiatives will be associated with the core domains: curriculum and instruction, technology, school culture and climate, professional development, family and community partnerships, and, yes, data analysis. All of the new efforts should advance the schoolwide goal.

For each initiative undertaken, action teams should have established one or more indicators of success. Some indicators refer to data that is already collected at the school level—perhaps student attendance—and the goal may be specific: student absences will

Figure 7.1   Fishbone Root-Cause Analysis

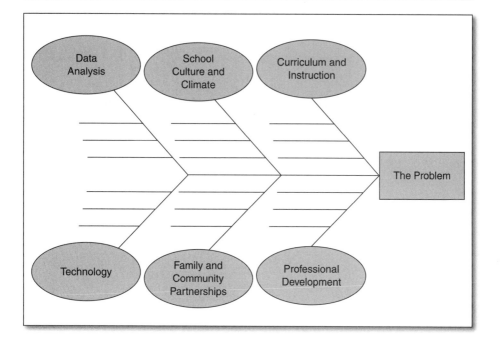

decrease by 10 percent. Others may have some level of ambiguity—
such as "student achievement will increase"—and need some collection of new data or organization of existing data. It is not the
responsibility of the Data Analysis Action Team to recommend a specification of what will count as an increase in student achievement,
but it is its responsibility to help the guiding coalition determine what
should be measured, how often, and with what comparisons.

What should be measured? School improvement plans often include
goals about improving communication with parents. Action team
indicators should help specify what that should look like in terms
of impact: Will they consider it a success if more teachers report
communication with individual parents? What about parents'
perceptions? What is available for comparison of previous
activity? Data Analysis Action Teams should help the guiding

coalition determine what existing data may be used to evaluate the impact of new initiatives and what new data might be collected to improve the understanding of their impact.

What points of reference are most relevant? Some behavior-related indicators are seasonal. Most obvious might be attendance. Winters bring flu. Spring may require a few days of extra vacation. It would be misleading, then, to compare rates of absenteeism in the fall with those rates in the winter. Rather, comparisons need to be made with equivalent contexts. In this case, rates of absenteeism are best compared with the same period in the previous year.

How often should data on outcomes be made available? Some objectives are best met with frequent observations. When one anticipates a relatively quick shift in behavior and the strategies employed in the initiative can be easily adjusted, frequent observations are extremely helpful. Procedures in the lunchroom are an easy example of such. Such trend data are absolutely essential for making midcourse adjustments.

On the other hand, some objectives will take more time to achieve than others. Any effort, for instance, to reduce the likelihood that students drop out will take more than a year and require some intermediate indicators, such as attendance records of students who are at risk. The Data Analysis Action Team can help the guiding coalition by providing some alternative indicators and possible schedules for collecting the relevant data.

What time span should be associated with assessing impact? Whether or not a new initiative has its intended impact depends, in part, on the time parameters set for the assessment. Renowned scholars, superintendents, and politicians routinely commit the fatal error of evaluating the impact of new policies, technologies, or interventions over much too short a time span. Ecologists routinely complain, for instance, that laboratory studies of the impact of environmental changes on the life cycle or sustainability of plants and animals establish a time frame for the study far short of when one would expect to see an effect on them. Adopting new technologies in schools has a similar problem with the span of time within which teachers as well as administrators anticipate an impact. The Data Analysis Action Team may be able to provide some guidance by investigating similar efforts that are well documented.

CONCLUSION

In our discussion of data analysis, we first sought to understand why teachers often report that data fail to inform their instructional decisions. We propose three factors to explain the problems: Most teachers lack access to data about the students they are currently teaching or those they recently taught. The data teachers most often review are aggregated using a format that mixes relevant and irrelevant data. Aggregated data requires that one address far more statistical issues than might arise in looking at individual student data.

We reviewed how the Data Analysis Action Team might support a school's effort to

- improve student learning,
- conduct deeper investigations into the root cause of persistent problems, and
- evaluate the impact of new initiatives.

Improving student learning: To improve student learning, anticipating greater availability of individual student data from diagnostic or formative assessments and annual state assessments, we explored how the data might address three instructional questions:

- Which students are struggling?
- How might struggling students be grouped to target instruction?
- What activities work best for which students?

Aggregate achievement data offer educators important insights into persistent problems. With proper comparisons, they allow educators to focus on the likely source of learning issues— in particular, determining whether the problems may be found by evaluating curriculum alignment issues or instructional issues.

Conducting root-cause analysis: To conduct root-cause analysis, the Data Analysis Action Team supports all teams in their efforts to determine root causes of persistent problems. To begin the investigation, the team provides trend data on the problem. As possible root causes are evaluated, it provides data that will help a team validate (or reject) the likely link between the problem and the likely causes.

Evaluating the impact of new initiatives: To evaluate the impact of new initiatives, in addition to helping the guiding coalition identify existing and new data that will measure the impact of new initiatives, the Data Analysis Action Team helps determine the time span in which to anticipate an impact, the relevant points of comparison, and the frequency with which interim reports on the indicators should be available.

In all instances, the Data Analysis Action Team seeks to provide data that can be interpreted easily and responsibly by their colleagues.

CHAPTER EIGHT

Family and Community Partnerships

T he needs of students and teachers drive the type of partnerships that should be established with parents and community
organizations. While this seems obvious, all too often schools focus
on activities that, at best, have marginal effects on school goals.
Take, for instance, an effort to increase attendance at parent-
teacher association meetings—a good and noble goal. Yet, most
educators understand that the students in greatest need of family
support are the least likely to have parents in attendance at such
meetings. Similarly, we often recruit business partners without any
consideration of what school needs they can address. It is the responsibility of the Family and Community Partnerships Action Team to help
its school find ways in which these relationships can be integral to
meeting school goals. The team should not attempt to develop and
implement projects that address both family and community partnerships in the same year.

In the first part of this chapter, we identify those aspects of
parent involvement that researchers find make a difference in
student learning and discuss ways in which schools can encourage such support. We also explore ways in which parent communities can help address a problem perceived by both parents and

educators—that of student self-discipline. The second part of the chapter provides an overview of the ways in which schools have engaged business and community organizations to support student learning—a topic with meager research evidence, but from our experience an untapped resource for schools. We also provide illustrations of successful school partnerships with health and social service organizations.

FAMILY PARTNERSHIPS

When it comes to parents, Goldilocks's frustration with her visit to the home of the three bears comes to mind. Parent involvement is seldom "just right." Often it is way too much, other times, way too little. Finding a "just right" relationship is hard. Unfortunately, parents with high degrees of involvement in their child's education can sometimes undermine their child's interest in learning more than parents who demonstrate no interest. It's difficult for educators to identify appropriate ways to help either type of parent. In this section, we attempt to identify, first, what types of parent involvement make the biggest difference in student learning and then suggest ways in which educators can partner with parents.

Establishing the Essentials

Assessing trust: Partnerships rest on trusting relationships. Before the Family and Community Partnerships Action Team frames the issues it would like to address, team members should understand the level of trust existing between parents and educators at the school. Does trust exist, or must it be cultivated? Whether the action team considers it appropriate to target all students or those most at risk, a strategy for improving parental support must begin by ensuring that trusting relations exist between parents and educators.

Indicators of parents' trust of educators include the degree to which parents believe the following:

- This school provides a welcoming environment.
- My child is treated with respect and dignity at school.

- Teachers care about my child's success.
- Teachers welcome my feedback about difficulties my child is experiencing.

Indicators of teachers' trust of parents include the degree to which teachers believe the following:

- Talking with parents helps me understand my students better.
- Staff at this school work hard to build trusting relationships.
- Most of my students' parents support my teaching efforts.
- Most of my students' parents do their best to help their children learn. (Adapted from Bryk & Schneider, 2002)

Building trust: Researchers have yet to give much attention to the types of communication that create the biggest impact on parents' trust; however, practitioners' recommendations are consistent with our more general understanding of methods for creating trust.

Teachers can demonstrate an active interest in their students' welfare and that they care about their success. Are teachers' initial contacts with a parent providing good news about a student's performance? E-mail, cell phones, or even handwritten notes can be used to provide compliments about students' ideas, academic efforts, or acts of good citizenship. Some teachers in elementary schools keep their cell phones handy to leave messages for parents and some even maintain a log of calls or notes to parents with the goal of ensuring that parents receive some supportive message at least once a month.

Once educators demonstrate that they are an advocate and admirer of a parent's son or daughter, discussions about misbehavior or a missed assignment will go much smoother. Trust enables the parent to become a cooperative partner with the teacher as they work toward the common interest of the student.

Building trust requires schools to communicate in a timely way the types of information parents value. A recent study of adolescents' parents found that they were most interested in attending workshops on how to develop the talents and skills of their children. As part of their study for Public Agenda, John Bridgeland and his colleagues (2008) surveyed parents on their perception of American high schools. Slightly over 50 percent of the parents reported that it would be "extremely helpful" to ensure that they know what their child needs for success—particularly rigorous courses and skill sets required for admission to and success in college. Parents with children attending low-performing schools were more likely than the average parent to report that it would be "extremely helpful" to provide more flexibility in scheduling parent-teacher meetings for full-time workers.

Sandra Christensen's (2004) meta-analysis of studies on parent-school partnerships identified a number of structural and psychological barriers to developing strong parent-school partnerships (see Table 8.1). While trust is listed separately, many of the barriers may be viewed as reasons why trust fails to develop. Researchers have been unable to prioritize the most important factors, but clearly all school staff play an important role in building meaningful partnerships.

Parents Providing Academic Support

Helping with schoolwork: When it comes to parents helping students learn, incongruities between teacher expectations and parent behavior exist. Public Agenda and the National Comprehensive Center for Teacher Quality (2007) surveyed parents and teachers about homework and found some striking differences: Almost 60 percent of the teachers surveyed expected parents to check homework every night. On the other hand, only 17 percent of the surveyed parents reported that they do so.

Can educators increase the involvement of parents in their child's homework? What is the evidence that it will make a difference? As of 2005, the U.S. Census Bureau estimates that 78 percent of mothers with school-age children are in the workforce. If both parents are working, homework may be especially challenging. Even parent interest in monitoring homework may be problematic, as 50 percent of the parents reported having had a serious confrontation with their children about homework that resulted in crying or yelling (Public Agenda & NCCTQ, 2007). Tired parents, hoping for some quality time with their children, likely take a pass on monitoring homework. Should educators continue to press for more parent support and involvement in school assignments?

Research on the effectiveness of parents helping or monitoring homework suggests educators may need to reassess their expectations—especially compared to the positive effects of

Table 8.1 Barriers to Developing School-Parent Relationships

Structural Barriers

Limited contact for building trust

Limited time for communication and meaningful dialogue

Communication occurring primarily during crises

Limited contact for building trust within the family-school relationship

Limited skills and knowledge about how to collaborate

Lack of a routine communication system

Limited understanding of the constraints faced by the other partner

Psychological Barriers

Partial resistance toward increasing home-school cooperation

Lack of belief in a partnership orientation in parent-school relationships

A blaming and labeling attitude

Conflicts driven by a win-lose rather than a win-win attitude

Anger-provoking behaviors personalized by the other individual

Differences in parent-educator perspectives about children's performance

Cultural differences that are not understood

Limited skills in seeing the perspective of the other

Knowledge of child limited to one environment

Failure to view differences as strengths

Low interest preserving the family-school relationship across time

---

Source: Adapted from Christensen, 2004.

school-based involvement (attending teacher-parent conferences, volunteering in classrooms, attending school events) and engaging in general intellectual activities (reading with them or visiting museums). Eva Pomerantz and her colleagues (2007) reviewed the results from over 300 studies of parent involvement with schoolwork and discovered a split between negative and positive effects on student achievement.

The wrong type of parent-student interactions, Pomerantz and her colleagues conclude, actually *reduces* students' engagement with school and effort in learning. Students' interest and performance in school is most likely to decrease when parents conduct drill sergeant supervision over their children, when they control when and how homework gets done, and—worst of all—when they make references to their children's ability, or lack thereof. In each of these cases, school becomes a "downer" for the children—reminding them of those negative experiences. First and foremost, then, what parents do to support their children's education needs to enhance, not undermine, a child's interest in school.

Table 8.2 summarizes Pomerantz and her colleagues' (2007) framework for parent-child interactions that can have a positive effect on students' performance. If educators hope to realize positive results from parent involvement, they need to ensure that parent interactions lack negativity, support student autonomy, and focus compliments on effort rather than ability.

Parents whose high school age children attend low-performing schools differ remarkably from parents at high-performing schools in their perception of how well high schools involve parents in their child's education and planning for future education opportunities. Perhaps the most striking differences are not the most profound: While the biggest gaps occur with the opportunities parents have to be involved in their child's education, the most important differences, it seems, are those related to postsecondary education. Only 20 to 40 percent of surveyed parents with children attending low-performing high schools report that schools do a good job of providing information about graduation requirements, college opportunities, and the like; yet, it's likely these are the parents who most likely lack such information. Most parents, regardless of income, consider going to college very important—Latino and African American parents more so than Whites not of Latino origin.

Marginal students' high school attendance and graduation rates are higher when parents see the connection between their children's current behavior and what they can do after graduation. In one study, school administrators invited representatives of various technical schools and community colleges to make a series of presentations to parents on the career opportunities (and salaries) realized from associate degrees and certificates granted by their institutions. Carefully linking those opportunities to high school performance (not always easy), educators were able to help parents link current student behavior to future opportunities that they could envision for their children. Researchers observed a statistically significant increase in student attendance and school completion following that intervention. They concluded that parents would be more active—or

Table 8.2   Parent Motivational Strategies and Student Success

Strategy Questions	*Examples*
Do parents support and nurture their children's autonomy in learning?	• Parents help children develop their own schedule for doing homework. • Parents ask questions that help their child choose a research project.
Do parents focus on the process of learning and the efficacy of effort (versus innate ability)?	• Parents help children think about strategies for mastering some skills.
Do parents communicate their enthusiasm for school and show support for their efforts?	• When listening to their child's account of the day at school, parents show support and interest in their child's experiences.
Do parents communicate their confidence in their child's potential?	• Parents express confidence in their child's potential to do well on assignments or tests.

Source: Adapted from Pomerantz, Moorman, & Litwack, 2007.

even intrusive—in their students' daily decisions, if they saw the link to opportunities that were on the horizon with the daily decisions of their adolescents (Pomerantz et al., 2007).

Parent and educator roles in developing student self-discipline: When it comes to deciding where to teach, vast majorities of both elementary and secondary teachers would choose schools where supportive parents and student behavior were significantly better over those schools that had significantly higher pay (Public Agenda & NCCTQ, 2007). What it means to have "supportive parents" necessarily differs among teachers, but when it comes to issues of student behavior in classrooms, most teachers would begin with students' need for more self-control and self-discipline.

These concerns are valid. The famous marshmallow experiment suggests that acquiring self-discipline may be one of the more important strategies for improving the quality of life for both educators and students. In the 1960s, Walter Mischel, a professor then at Stanford University, studied four-year-olds' ability to delay gratification. Each was given one marshmallow and promised another one when the assistant returned if they could wait until the assistant returned to eat the first one. Some children could wait and others could not. Some 15 years later, when these same children were adolescents, those who had the ability to wait as four-year-olds were better adjusted and more dependable (determined via surveys of their parents and teachers), and scored, on average, 250 points higher on the Scholastic Aptitude Test. Notably, Mischel later found that easily explained tactics allowed children who had waited very short periods to wait for quite long periods (Mischel et al., 1989; Mischel & Ayduk, 2004). Numerous other studies confirm these earlier findings.

The lack of self-control usually is attributed to inadequate parenting. While students' misbehavior results from a complex set of circumstances—everything from hunger, stress, learning disabilities, or traumatic encounters in and out of school, both parents and teachers have significant roles in improving student behavior. Increasingly, researchers link defiant behavior in a classroom to taunts or other forms of bullying that the child encounters at school.

Regardless of the source of the behavioral problems, parents see the need for improving self-discipline and self-control in ways very similar to teachers. Steve Farkas and his colleagues (2002) report the results of a parent survey sponsored by Public Agenda. Parents were asked what character values are absolutely essential to teach their children and whether they thought they had succeeded in teaching them. Table 8.3 shows the results.

Of greatest interest, 83 percent of parents considered it "absolutely essential" for children to learn self-control and self-discipline, but only 34 percent thought they had succeeded in teaching these values to their children. Thus, over half of those who felt teaching their children self-control and self-discipline was "absolutely essential" thought they had not succeeded. Given that educators and parents share the same concerns, is it possible for teachers to be coconspirators with parents? Two approaches appear especially interesting. First, consider strategies for students taking more ownership of their educational goals. For instance, Minke and Anderson (as cited in Elias, Bryan, Patrikakou, & Weissberg, 2003) were interested in converting parent-teacher conferences into more meaningful and productive events and coincidentally increasing student commitments:

> The conference was restructured to begin with written preparation by all participants: teachers, parents, and the student list

Table 8.3 Parent Perceptions of School's Consultation

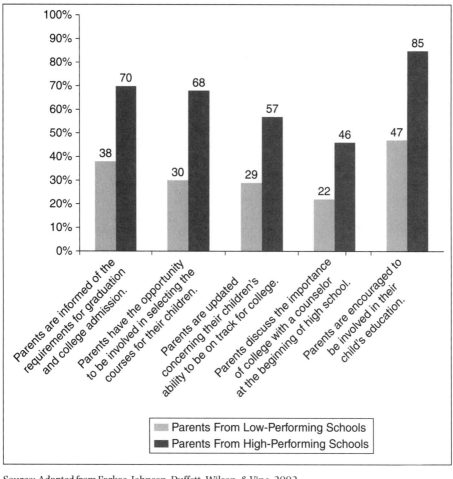

Source: Adapted from Farkas, Johnson, Duffett, Wilson, & Vine, 2002.

strengths, areas needing improvement, other goals, and questions. At the meeting, the child introduces all participants and then begins the discussion of strengths, moving into other areas. The group makes decisions about priorities for further work, plans are made, a follow-up time is set, and then an evaluation process is outlined so that all parties will know the extent to which progress is made. Following such a process made teachers' perceptions of parents more positive. (p. 145)

To us, though, much more happens at such a conference. Student motivation likely increases and a framework for self-discipline becomes operational in a setting where the student has a voice. Parents and teachers share expectations and share a commitment with the student to reach the goals. Teachers and parents have a fresh context in which to know and understand the child. Finally, both the parents and teachers have reasons to contact the other.

A second approach to cultivating self-discipline emerges from the work of Elias and his colleagues (2003). They focus on significant needs of all adolescents as they develop their identities: belonging, contribution, appreciation, confidence, and competencies. Contribution, they conclude, is the most crucial. "Teens thrive on helping or making contributions to causes—saving the environment, helping senior citizens, working in soup kitchens . . ." (Elias et al., 2003, p. 139). Schools can be an important vehicle—partnering with a variety of agencies in their area—in creating such opportunities. Returning to the primary concern of parents and teachers: "contributions" cultivate students' sense of self-efficacy, teach planning skills, and give students the opportunity to understand the consequences of their actions—all integral factors to self-discipline.

Parents Work in Schools

Studies show that parent volunteering in kindergarten and early grades predicts student success in upper grades, but researchers have yet to determine whether this is a function of the time parents are available for such service, a powerful communicator of parents' priorities, or whether parents' presence at this stage creates a sense of comfort and familiarity that helps students develop a positive orientation toward school.

A little over a third of the parents surveyed by Farkas and colleagues (2002) say one or more of the following about their parenting:

- There's so much stress in my life that being a parent can be overwhelming.
- I'm sometimes too tired to be firm with my child even when I know I should.
- I sometimes let too many things go.

Can schools help tired or stressed-out parents? They can help foster parent-to-parent networks to provide moral support and sometimes even needed resources. Helping to build stronger relations *among* parents appears to increase the confidence parents have in setting limits with adolescents and creates a more coherent set of expectations among students in a school (Coleman, 1990). The old expression "Does your mother know what you are doing?" is an indica-

> Teenagers need to be contributors more than consumers, and belong more than buy (Elias et al., 2003).

tor of a time when all adults in a child's life were tightly knit together—as neighbors, members of the same church or synagogue, or fellow workers. While adults are more reticent to ask that question of children today, just the presence of someone who knows one's parents can have a similar effect.

That said, parents are more challenged than ever in getting to know their neighbors, much less those whose children play with their own. School functions that allow parents to work together—rather than just watch a performance or talk with a teacher—provide important opportunities for building relations among parents. Parents volunteering as part of a "fix-up" day at the school building or grounds or sharing booster club activities for sports or music groups provides them with the opportunity to create these valuable networks.

Parents' Voice in School Life

Perhaps the most common mistake made by policymakers is assuming that parents want and should be involved in school governance. Surveys of parents consistently find that they are least interested and least comfortable in roles related to school governance. Most states and districts, however, require parental involvement in school governance—with varying degrees of authority and usefulness. Shulamit Ritblatt and fellow researchers (2002) estimate 5 to 6 percent of parents become involved in school governance, and Pomerantz and colleagues (2007) conclude the impact on student learning is small. We have little evidence of the value of such formal roles for parents. On the other hand, parents do want to be consulted about their children's education.

Educators should use a variety of strategies to gain advice or input from all parents. National surveys (Public Agenda, 2002) repeatedly show that while most parents do not feel comfortable holding a role in school governance, they appreciate the opportunity to provide suggestions and recommendations about school operations. Many districts now have annual surveys of parents that allow educators to understand how parents view their school. Parents should have multiple ways to contact teachers—now increasingly easy with various forms of electronic communication. Elementary school teachers may even find Twitter a useful way to let parents know when something may have been upsetting to their children— their classroom rabbit may have died unexpectedly or one of their classmate's mother was in a serious accident.

In summary, both parents and teachers realize the value of cultivating students with self-discipline and persistence, but parents report disappointment in their success as parents in this regard. Pomerantz and colleagues' analysis of what type of parent support increases student learning gives us good hints about what is likely missing. Parents' interactions with their child should reflect a positive disposition toward school, support student effort over ability, and encourage autonomy in completing school assignments (Pomerantz et al., 2007). It's clear that parents, particularly those in high-poverty schools, hunger for information about how their children should prepare for postsecondary and future career opportunities.

Table 8.4 provides a reflection tool this action team may use to assess the school's existing level of engagement with families. Comparing a school's profile with its goals will help the team target the greatest opportunities to make a difference. In those more serious circumstances, where little trust appears to exist between educators and parents, an outside facilitator can help the team plan a strategy for improving the situation.

COMMUNITY PARTNERSHIPS

Community partnerships begin with need, marry need to imagination, and hope that boldness will lead to matrimony. Community collaboration can address some core challenges that educators face, particularly in middle schools. The type of collaboration established will vary depending on school goals, the size of the community, and the types of students served. Community collaboration can be useful in improving children's readiness to learn.

Table 8.4 Profile of Existing Family-School Relationships

1. Teachers' knowledge of home and work situations that affect family involvement.
2. Types of teacher-initiated contacts with families.
3. Notification strategies for student absenteeism or poor performance.
4. Parents' electronic access to students' attendance records, assignments, and test scores.
5. Expectations teachers have for parent involvement in schoolwork.
6. Programs available for parents to learn about postsecondary opportunities and requirements.
7. Parent participation in PTO, family nights, and parent-teacher conferences.
8. Opportunities for parents as volunteers.
9. Family participation rates in volunteer activities.
10. Opportunities for parents and teachers to be coconspirators in improving student behavior and motivation.

Attendance and behavior problems are often linked to health problems that physical and mental health services can provide.

Partnerships With Businesses

Often, schools acquire a partnership with a local business that has no specific purpose linked to student learning. Whatever the business offers will be okay—old computers, volunteer tutors, or free coffee and soft drinks for staff meetings. In our experience, schools and business organizations find these relationships disappointing. Within a year or so, the partnership is limited to businesses giving permission to have their company listed in the annual school improvement plan. Good partnerships, though, should be mutually beneficial.

Prior to considering any partnerships with local businesses, the Family and Community Partnerships Action Team needs to consult with the principal regarding existing partnerships the school has with local businesses and district policies for such partnerships.

Strategies for Success in School-Business Partnerships

- Make strategic matches that advance a school's improvement goals.
- Set clear expectations for school and businesses.
- Provide training for school staff and business employees.
- Create a meaningful process for communicating about the program and recognizing the contributions of business partners.
- Regularly monitor and evaluate each partnership and the overall program.

Adapted from
Daniels Fund, 2005

District policies differ radically. Some have central office coordinators who manage all school relationships with businesses, ensuring that major firms are not overwhelmed by requests for assistance. Some districts have school foundations that match school needs to interested businesses. At the other extreme, some districts encourage any and all school initiatives to build relationships with local businesses.

Some existing support from businesses may be invisible to teachers—perhaps they finance a specific program or provide support services for a computer lab. Careful consultation with the school's principal will ensure that the team is aware of current policies and relationships.

For partnerships to be worthwhile, schools should have a specific and important need that a business or community organization can help accomplish. A PreK–4 school in the urban northeastern United States decided one year that improving school readiness should be one of their major goals. Given that most parents of present and future students lived within eight to ten blocks of the school, they decided to target neighborhood businesses to help educate and engage parents. Many parents, as recent immigrants, knew little of the resources available to support their children.

First, team members identified a place that most parents frequented. In this case, it was a locally owned laundromat. Second, they identified key resources they wanted to introduce: the neighborhood library and health clinic. The laundromat owner embraced their idea and offered to raffle free dryer time. Librarians were delighted to come on Saturdays to read to young children and sign parents up for library cards. A health clinic staff person, accompanied by bilingual parents, explained inoculations the young children needed. With librarians sitting on blankets outside the laundromat reading to children, parents and their children were drawn to the place. Over the years, small shopkeepers around the neighborhood began to learn about the school's goals and identify ways in which they could help.

With a targeted need, school teams may seek out businesses for particular instructional challenges that result in long-term partnerships. Some years ago, an elementary school team sought to use an interdisciplinary unit on construction. The unit relied upon architecture to link history, science, and art. One of the culminating activities involved students experimenting with weight bearing structures—using only 3 × 5" cards and paper clips. Fear of failure dampened the teachers' enthusiasm: they didn't feel comfortable explaining the science concepts involved. At our suggestion, they sought assistance from a local architectural firm. Two young architects came for a visit, reviewed the proposed experiment, and readily agreed to help. They led the students through the set of experiments with a few additional props—including pictures of local buildings that illustrated different periods in their city's history. That day was only the beginning of what became a long-term relationship with the multiage classroom.

Local businesses can also make meaningful contributions to student learning by helping students to understand the applications of mathematics or science in their profession—providing concrete experiences with tools of their trade, or simply encouraging students to prepare themselves for careers in their field.

Many schools or districts have instituted routine visits (or systems of referrals) for basic health diagnostics (vision, hearing, dental, etc.). If this is absent, then it is worthwhile for a school to approach local clinics or medical and dental associations for a strategy of support. An elementary school in New York City realized that many of its educational challenges were made greater by the health problems of the families it served. Seeking some community support, the school established a social service consortium. Initially, it was merely a vehicle to refer obvious needs to appropriate agencies. By the end of their second meeting, though, social service agencies began to exchange information on shifting patterns (of need in the neighborhood), such as emergency room needs as well as new services available to families. (Judges began holding juvenile court hearings in the neighborhood.) Teachers learned to identify possible vision problems and became more confident in linking parents with agencies that could help with emotional trauma. Teachers attributed much of the students' academic success to their ability to address health and behavioral problems as well as the unflappable commitment parents had to the school.

Partnerships With Community-Based Organizations

Milbrey McLaughlin (2000) documents the myriad of community-based organizations that motivate youth and focus on students acquiring skills and knowledge. Successful ones—those that attract young people and make a difference—"are concentrated, focused, and disciplined in their approach to deepening students' skills and competence" (p. 10). Whether it's dance, sports, or community service, the successful programs are demanding of students and impact their academic and social competencies.

McLaughlin reports:

> Even hard-driving sports organizations find ways to broaden the perspectives and competencies of youth. For example, it is common in many organizations for team members to come to practice early to work with volunteers on homework, study for exams, or fine-tune specialized units related to their sport. Many coaches work academics into topics of great interest to their young athletes, such as nutrition and weight training. One year a basketball team had six-week units of study on the following topics: finances of the National

Volunteers From a Local College?

Teachers at a school were struggling to introduce the life of ancient Greece at their school—after all, neither their school nor their university experience had given any attention to ancient civilizations. Then someone remembered: ah yes, the classics professor at one of the local colleges. Let's face it, the professor was startled. He'd never been invited to a middle school. His enthusiasm was hard to contain—not only did he give teachers a quick immersion into the themes and lessons of the ancient civilization, but he also assigned his students the task of helping teachers develop some activities that could enable students to experience life in ancient Greece.

Basketball Association, physics in the sport of basketball, and neurophysiology. Each of these units included original research, problem sets, discussions of ethics, and decision-making. For example, the unit on the NBA covered costs of health insurance, uniforms, travel, income from ticket sales, taxes on players' salaries, and using probability theory to illustrate the youngsters' chances of making it to the NBA. The neurophysiology unit discussed steroids, heart rate under exertion, heat dehydration, and myths surrounding "chocolate highs" and "carbohydrate loading." (p. 11–12)

Struggling students benefit greatly from such experiences. Educators can revitalize a student's engagement with school if they cast a broad net over their community organizations. Researchers as far back as the 1960s consistently find that one of the best predictors of whether a young person will defy the odds and survive a dysfunctional family and neighborhood is to have one adult who cares passionately about the youth's welfare and is there to help dodge the risks and seize opportunities. McLaughlin (2000) and Sheldon (2007) find the same.

McLaughlin (2000) recommends that schools take the following actions to support community-based organizations serving young people:

Community-Based Organizations

- YMCA
- Birding associations
- Building associations
- Conservation societies
- Craft unions
- Fire associations
- Historical societies
- Museums
- Music groups
- Police associations
- Public libraries
- Veterans of Foreign Wars

- Recognize and reward youth for their participation in youth organizations.
- Include youth organizations as integral parts of strategies to improve learning.
- Help youth organizations assess the impact of their work on student performance in school.
- Provide incentives for teachers to learn about their students' work in youth organizations.
- Develop curricula that integrate community resources for learning and teaching.

It helps to take a quick inventory of community resources. Does the community have a historical society—who is its leader? Is there an association of architects that teachers might be able to contact? What local businesses and public services can be found nearby? Creating such a list might be an appropriate project for a parents' association or even a service project for a high school student.

CONCLUSION

The research reviewed in this chapter suggests that parents and teachers have a similar concern—the need for students to acquire self-discipline and perseverance—but priority given to parental involvement in homework differs.

Research on parental involvement suggests that

- parent presence at school in the early grades is an important predictor of students' future school success;
- positive communications between educators and parents establishes the trust needed to collaborate in solving problems with student behavior or performance;
- parents need guidance on effective ways to support their students' learning;
- strong networks among parents can increase their confidence in setting limits; and
- parents want a voice in their children's education, but most do not want a role in school governance.

Community and business partnerships should clearly connect to improving student learning by

- increasing students' understanding of academic concepts,
- improving health of students, or
- enhancing students' engagement with school.

Our experience suggests that initiating potential partnerships should begin with a limited task and timeframe that is clearly focused on a school's improvement goals. McLaughlin (2000) encourages schools to support student participation in community organizations that motivate them and focus on skill development.

CHAPTER NINE

Curriculum and Instruction

Each year, state and district policies result in greater restrictions on instruction—not just through academic standards, but also through pacing guides and interim assessments. It's easy to forget the frustrations of the 1990s when academic standards and state assessments might not even form a Venn diagram.

Since the inception of standardized testing, the most important predictor of student learning was *what* was taught. The press to move state assessments from "guess what's important" to strong alignment between published academic standards and state assessments has, thankfully, removed many frustrations. Yet, the new federal expectation that interim and baseline assessments be available throughout the year necessarily requires pacing guides aligned with them. Educators feel pressed even further to narrow their focus—sometimes making it even more difficult for struggling students to succeed.

In this context, the Curriculum and Instruction Action Team develops cross-curricular initiatives to increase the likelihood that students will grasp fundamental concepts and acquire fluency in essential skills in a variety of disciplines, such as making inferences or evaluating evidence. Their efforts not only should improve students' understanding and skills, but also reduce the likelihood that students will forget things they've been taught and require reteaching.

With this objective, we suggest that the team focus on three aspects of instructional practice that cross-curricular work can improve: the use of multiple modalities in instruction, the application of concepts or skills in multiple contexts, and the development of metacognitive skills. Each of these basic instructional needs can have a greater impact through some coordination or collaboration across subject areas. When students spontaneously identify the parallels from other classes, they not only reflect serious engagement, but also the integrative experiences that will improve their long-term "remembering" and ability to apply concepts to new and novel problems.

The Curriculum and Instruction Action Team should begin by reviewing all types of data, including state assessments and subjects not included on state assessments as well as reports by teachers. Educators who focus in the arts may review state or national standards to identify areas where their students experience difficulty to inform their instruction. Subscale scores in state assessments in mathematics and reading will be especially helpful in identifying crosscutting issues.

OPPORTUNITIES FOR COLLABORATION AND COORDINATION

Multiple modalities: Educators frequently incorporate multiple modalities into their lessons—using visual, auditory, and tactile strategies to help diverse learners acquire a better understanding of concepts. Some difficult concepts, though, may require some collaboration with educators in other subjects. Improving our ability to educate diverse learners, an important component of the federal Response to Intervention (RTI) program, will require that educators dig deeper for collaborative efforts to use multiple modalities.

Jane Burke's (2009) approach in a chemistry class provides an unusual illustration of collaboration between specialists and classroom teachers. Burke invited a dance instructor to join her chemistry class and choreograph a dance illustrating a "double bond." Students explained chemical reactions to the dance instructor who kept the queries going, "Why does that happen? How?" A student reported that the experience had at least "temporarily erased" her mental block. Another student reported, "Now when I think of 'double bond,' I visualize it" (Burke, 2009, p. 10). The dance experiment provided Burke with a gratifying surprise: she discovered a student's hidden talent for dance. He was a student who, heretofore, had been totally disengaged in the class. On this occasion, he took charge of the session several times to suggest movements that would represent various chemical reactions.

Creating a dance to illustrate various chemical reactions exemplifies the general principle cognitive scientists extract from their research: learners are more likely to remember and understand what they've learned when educators illustrate a concept in multiple modalities. Equally important, the understandings students acquire with these different approaches enable them to apply what they've learned in novel situations. When the mind has had the opportunity to approach a concept through multiple modalities, the learning is imprinted much more deeply and builds multiple connections to the concept.

High school science teachers sought to be more inclusive in their biology classes but realized that their lesson plans would need some modification. Collaboration between a biology instructor and special education teacher led to some surprising results. Working on a genetics unit, the two decided to act out the outcomes with dominant and recessive genes, complete with costumes. The results surprised them: not only did those students with more serious learning disabilities grasp the concept, but marginal students performed much better with this approach. Combining the instructional wisdom of special education teachers with the conceptual knowledge of content teachers can transform the effectiveness of instruction for many students.

Using student performance data, especially of struggling students, will help the action team identify targets for teacher collaborations that should improve students' understanding of core concepts in a subject.

Multiple contexts: Educators know the value of providing multiple contexts for the application of a concept or application of a skill within their own subject. For many students, though, it is critical that they have the opportunity to work with a concept or apply a skill in a subject they find highly engaging. This is an opportunity for coordinating across subjects. The Curriculum and Instruction Action Team provides a venue in which such coordination can occur.

Take, for instance, the skills needed to make appropriate inferences, a valuable skill in all subjects, even sports. Data from a variety of sources suggest that American students lack such skills. The action team most likely will identify weaknesses in making inferences from the reading proficiency scores, but it is likely that most educators have seen this deficiency in their own classes. For instance, adolescent students usually discard competing accounts of the past with the claim: "That's just one opinion versus another." Peter Lee (2005) argues that once students can distinguish between relics and records as well as between intentional and unintentional evidence, they overcome this disregard for historical accounts.

The Value of Multiple Contexts

If you're old enough to remember paper (rather than electronic) files, you often experienced some frustration in finding materials you wanted. Suppose you organized your picture albums by the year the pictures were taken. Today, you want to find pictures of your niece. It's her 21st birthday and you want to make her a scrapbook. You cannot just enter "my favorite niece" onto a search engine. You have only one link to the photos. You spend all day going through your albums year by year, page by page.

Often our brains function as primitively as those old photo albums: only one way to access what we know. Most of us have a wealth of information in our brain, but access facts or procedures with only one stimulus or link. Consider the last time you watched a quiz show. A question stumps you. Once you hear the answer, you mumble: "I knew that!" Unfortunately, you've likely bumped into an instance where you have only one "link" to the knowledge—just like the one link to your niece's pictures. When we encounter problems recalling what we think we know in a timely way, we're experiencing what cognitive scientists call *inert* knowledge: we know it, but we cannot retrieve it. Just as we use technology to access our photos and other files in multiple ways, we need to build brains that have multiple links to what we know. Cognitive scientists refer to that ability as *transfer;* that is, can we transfer what we know to novel situations or problems?

Working with the same concept in multiple contexts builds multiple links for the application of the concept. It makes our brains more responsive and able to solve problems in new and novel situations.

The action team may choose a month-long coordination of activities related to inferences or they may find schoolwide activities, such as detective games in homerooms, as an appropriate approach. If coordinating across subjects, mathematics instructors may open classes with logic games; language arts teachers may complete a character analysis from one of their readings; and art teachers may ask students to guess the origins of a painting and explain the clues that led them to that conclusion.

Students' difficulties with rational numbers is legendary—and for a good reason. Confusion about them is the great barrier to success in algebra. Researchers consistently find that students incorrectly transfer knowledge of what they know about whole numbers to their interpretation of fractions. For instance, when comparing 8/16 to 3/4, students often conclude that 8/16 is greater simply because 8 is greater than 3 and 16 is greater than 4.

For the average student, there is little transparently rational about the way fractions and decimals work. If most educators are like us, they don't know that the term *rational number* refers to numbers in ratio forms, not the apparent logic embedded in them. Before we can even consider coordinating efforts with this challenge, then, it helps to change terminology: we are talking about *proportionality*.

The use of proportionality pervades all subjects: issues of scale in art and architecture, map reading in social studies, notation in music, and the consumer sciences can't do much without it. Coordinating the work in mathematics classes with some exposure to the concept in multiple contexts will inevitably allow many more students to become proficient with mathematical concepts.

The increasing problem with fractions likely reflects the incongruity between students' prior experiences and the sequence in which certain mathematical principles occur—a problem, again, that coordination across subjects may help solve. Joan Moss (2005) suggests that the introduction to rational numbers should begin with percentages since students today have greater exposure to them than fractions. She reports on a series of classroom experiments where teachers introduce the concept of percentages prior to introducing fractions. Students' grasp of concepts and ingenuity was superior when they began with the terminology and visuals associated with percentage compared to the traditional sequence beginning with fractions.

Children's prior experiences with proportionality has changed in the past one hundred years. In the early part of the twentieth century, many home activities involved measurements with fractional notations: cooking, sewing, building, and possibly even marking time (quarter-past, half-past on those face clocks). Now, we microwave dinner, add one cup of water to the brownie mix, and purchase prefab playhouses. Percentages are everywhere in the lives of children: clothing sales with 20 or 50 percent off, political polls giving a candidate a 15 percent lead, and a 9 percent sales tax are part of daily life.

Introducing proportionality—both as fractions and percentages—in a variety of subjects can be of tremendous value to students. A student's interest in music, but fear of math, may be the only means by which the student will grasp mathematical principles. Just drawing the parallels between music notation and fractions may be all it takes to open doors for a struggling student.

Feedback: Metacognitive skills refer to the ability to monitor one's own learning to determine what is making sense, what isn't, and how to "fix" the problem. Research suggests that specific strategies can facilitate these skills, which evolve in students over time.

Researchers find that even the best teachers rely on types of feedback that neither increase student motivation nor improve their metacognitive skills. John Hattie and Helen Timperley (2007) synthesized the results of over 6000 studies of the effects of teachers' feedback on student commitment to learning and actual achievement. Basic categories of feedback in their framework include four levels:

- *Task-oriented (or corrective) feedback* provides indications of how well the task is being accomplished. *(Is it correct or incorrect?)* Most teachers rely upon questions that lead to this type of feedback.
- *Process feedback* provides suggestions on how to improve the work. *(Try revising this document to reflect the basic components of solid reporting.)*
- *Self-regulating feedback* encourages students to evaluate their own work. *(You know about the elements of a good essay; review your work to see if you've incorporated them.)*
- *Self-oriented feedback* gives personal praise. *(You're a great student!)*

Hattie and Timperley (2007) find that teachers most often use task-oriented feedback and self-oriented feedback. While task-oriented feedback can have positive effects, self-oriented feedback does not. If a teacher combines both task-oriented and self-oriented feedback, any potential benefit is erased.

Telling a student that he or she is smart may be a sure way, in fact, to make them less smart. Carol Dweck studied the difference in student behavior if students were randomly told one of two things after working on a relatively easy puzzle: "You must be really smart" or "You must have worked really hard." In subsequent sessions, the students were given a choice of an "easy" puzzle or a hard one—although all received the same puzzles that were more difficult that the first ones. Ninety percent of the students who had been praised for their effort chose the harder puzzles. A majority of those who had been praised for their intelligence chose the easy test. Even more interesting, those who had been praised for effort got very involved and persisted in exploring different strategies. A third set of puzzles was offered later—all as easy as the first ones. Those who had been praised for effort did better than those whose praise was oriented toward their intelligence (as cited in Bronson, 2007).

Assisting students to reflect on their learning requires educators to increase their reliance on process feedback and self-regulating feedback. Both types of feedback are generally more powerful in terms of attaining student engagement and improving students' deeper understanding. Struggling students, however, are seldom motivated or capable of engaging in a review of their own work (that is, self-regulating feedback).

Smaller studies suggest that the problem may be even more pernicious. Likely responding to the perceived needs of students, teachers are more likely to give such self-oriented feedback (i.e., praise to lower performing students). Teachers' otherwise noble efforts may actually backfire. Making the issue even more complex, students arrive at school with different cultural norms about how and under what circumstances praise is given. For some cultures, public praise, for instance, is unacceptable and may generate embarrassment.

While specific metacognitive strategies that teachers use differ by subject, all of them share the stages of modeling, coaching, and scaffolding. Teachers model by talking through their own "internal conversations" regarding a problem in, for instance, science, or reading a text in history. Students attempt the same with coaching and scaffolding from the instructor. More sophisticated metacognitive actions occur as students mature as learners. For instance, older students should be able to assess what they need to do or know in order achieve a better understanding of the text and make plans to acquire that knowledge. Students acquire these skills slowly, but more consistently, if educators guide students in this type of self-reflection.

The value of teaching metacognitive skills can be seen rather quickly. Xiadong Lin and James Lehman (1999) demonstrate the value of reflective activities on students' subsequent ability to apply what they had learned to new situations. In their study of college students, they evaluated the effects of students' reflecting on what they were learning about the controlling of variables in a complex science experiment. As the students studied, some received periodic questions that asked them to reflect upon—and explain—what they were doing and why. Others did not receive those questions. Subsequently, the experimenters tested to determine if there was a difference in the two groups in terms of their ability to apply what they had learned to a new situation. Those given the reflection (metacognitive) tasks clearly outperformed those who had not been given those questions. Developing what many educators refer to as *wrappers* for each class session, homework, or exams requires students to reflect upon the task and improve their recall and understanding. Self-reflection also provides teachers with needed feedback on what needs to be addressed in future sessions.

In a massive review of the research on instructional feedback, John Hattie and Helen Timperley (2007) find feedback that cultivates a student's metacognitive skills has the strongest impact on student learning relative to praise, rewards, corrective responses, or punishment. Unfortunately, other studies (Bond, Jaeger, & Hattie, 2000) suggest that even our best educators rarely provide feedback that encourages students to reflect on their work.

A safe and stimulating environment, on the other hand, occurs when educators treat mistakes as a normal part of learning, perceive misconceptions as an opportunity for everyone to learn, and provide feedback that reflects an absolute goal rather than accomplishments relative to other students (Shepard, 2001; Stipek, 1996).

With mistakes, simple assurances—such as "Oh, that often happens the first time someone tries this," or "It's not unusual for someone to make that mistake"—allow students to see mistakes clearly, and, yet, sustain willingness to try again. Without such support, students lacking a strong history of success in school may be especially inclined to abandon making any effort. Students need to sense that their continued efforts will make a difference.

More important, mistakes provide educators with a window into what learners are thinking and give the particular instructor a deeper understanding of the learner's reasoning: "How did you arrive at that solution? What are the other things you tried?" With misconceptions, students need the opportunity to explain their reasoning, hear other students explain theirs, and discuss collaboratively underlying misconceptions or assumptions that might explain the difference. To do such, the environment must be emotionally safe.

A Curriculum and Instruction Action Team may find it helpful to support educators in developing more productive feedback strategies. Coordination with the Professional Development Action Team might result in specific schoolwide activities that allow educators to develop a variety of wrappers for their classroom instruction or to simply assess what types of feedback they wish to add to their repertoire.

OTHER OPPORTUNITIES FOR COLLABORATION AND SUPPORT

Engaging students: Most of the time, teachers engage students' interest by establishing links between new concepts, literature, or historical studies and their everyday lives. It's the emotional engagement that pulls students into deeper probing of a problem or challenge.

When teachers rely upon cultural icons (or local events) to engage students—popular television programs, school history or heroes, and the functioning of everyday objects or fundamental issues students confront in their daily lives—they not only create the emotional spark students need to dig into a problem or challenge, they also create ways in which students are able to build the connective tissue to transfer what they are learning to new and novel situations. Teachers often refer to the need to "hook" students into new concepts they introduce by connecting the discussion with their everyday lives—a need that becomes increasingly challenging in classrooms with students from diverse backgrounds.

Frankly, though, it is hard for teachers to stay abreast of the fads and heroes of their students. In our urban areas, any given group of students reflects as much cultural diversity as a United Nations meeting. In other contexts, such as rural areas, cultural understandings may be universal within the community, but not reflected in the expectations the state has for science or, perhaps, literature.

In some contexts, the Curriculum and Instruction Action Team may find it useful to help colleagues keep current of their students' interests and concerns. With the results of a student survey, the team may be able to use a faculty meeting to report on students' favorite TV shows, most popular band, sports they are playing after school, favorite store in the mall, the last movie seen in a theater, or perhaps the last book or magazine read. The action team could even prepare crib sheets for faculty about favorite TV shows or bands.

Healthy students: For some Curriculum and Instruction Action Teams, a focus on health-related curriculum and activities may be especially important. The Centers for Disease Control (CDC) reports that the number of obese children in upper elementary grades doubled in the past 25 years, reaching 17 percent in 2006. This means that some fifth and sixth graders actually experience high cholesterol, high blood pressure, type 2 diabetes, sleep apnea, and bone and joint problems (as cited in Daniels et al., 2005). CDC estimates that almost a third of the high schools in the United States lack any health or physical education requirements. According to the National Center for Education Statistics (2005), over 80 percent of public elementary schools provide daily recess periods for their students. The length of time, however, those students spend at recess declined substantially in the last 25 years. Obesity among young children has almost doubled during that same period.

What can make a difference? Diana Coyl (2009) encourages educators to focus on health education and prevention in the upper elementary grades, since older students are less responsive to adult advice. Physician researcher Romina Barros's research (as cited in Parker-Pope, 2009) on physical activity among third graders revealed that children with daily recess greater than 15 minutes are more likely to learn more and behave better than those with less recess. A similar study of middle school students found a positive correlation between enrollment in gym classes and academic performance. Barros argues that recess should be considered part of the curriculum: "We should understand that kids need that break because the brain needs that break" (as cited in Parker-Pope, 2009, par. 5).

Perhaps the most interesting evidence of the value of recess breaks comes from Andrea Taylor and Frances Kuo (2009). They studied the effects of various types of outdoor activities on the ability of children with attention deficit hyperactivity disorder (ADHD) between the ages of 7 and 12 to concentrate in school. Nature walks proved to be the clear winner over walks in neighborhoods and downtown. Nature walks, in fact, proved as efficacious as medications typically given to students diagnosed with ADHD.

The Curriculum and Instruction Action Team not only may need to assess what exercise opportunities can be made available for students, but the team may also wish to find ways to integrate more awareness of nutrition and healthy behaviors into the curriculum. Collaboration with the Family and Community Partnerships Action Team may help them expand the scope of opportunities for students' physical activity outside of school.

Developing appropriate support to prevent learning or behavioral challenges: For the past 20 years, researchers sought to discover ways to improve the performance of students with learning disabilities. Evidence accumulated that most learning disabilities could be prevented with strong reading programs, interim assessments, and targeted interventions if they were provided to students at the preschool and primary grades (Haager, Klingner, & Vaughn, 2007). Astonishingly, researchers find that if schools have strong reading programs and intervene with struggling students early, the number of students with learning disabilities could drop by more than half. While more difficult to achieve, struggling students in the upper grades can attain greater levels of proficiency with timely interventions that, similar to lower grades, provide targeted assistance in small groups or individual tutoring. Recovery in later grades—after frustration and embarrassment have taken their toll on a student's interest and confidence—will always remain more difficult.

The policies established by the new Individuals with Disabilities Act (IDEA, 2004) reflect the findings of this research. Prevention, as well as intervention, strategies follow a process known as response to intervention (RTI), which is, in essence, putting the evidence of research into operational forms; that is, how do we put what we know into practice? The RTI process, in practice, involves the following:

- All schools and classrooms use high-quality, scientifically sound, instructional programs and behavioral support systems.
- All schools monitor student learning and behavioral problems to identify those that may need some additional support or more careful assessments.
- Schools help regular classroom teachers in providing additional support to students that need it in the classroom—through alternative lessons or behavioral management strategies.
- Monitoring of efficacy of the support, as well as the response of the student, is continuous.
- If a student's problems persist, individual tutoring or other interventions out of the classroom may be provided and monitoring continues.
- Parent involvement is included at all stages.

As much as 15 percent of the federal IDEA funds available to a district may be allocated for these measures, designed to prevent learning and behavioral difficulties that permanently compromise the successful integration of students into regular classrooms. Schools are expected to use scientifically verified intervention strategies and establish a broad-based committee to monitor the progress of students experiencing learning difficulties. IDEA funds may now be used to support professional development for regular classroom teachers who work with preschool and primary grades and those at all grade levels who work with struggling students.

For the past decade, teachers sought to address the varied learning needs of students through differentiating instruction: class activities, assignments, and assessments included, ideally, distinct approaches for English language learners, students with

various learning disabilities, or those who needed more challenging assignments than most other students. As our understanding
of the diverse needs of students grew, the expectations for more
and more options for each classroom activity grew. From a
teacher's point of view, then, the expectations for any given lesson
grew increasingly complex.

The notion of a universal design for learning originally began
as an effort to help educators identify instructional activities or
strategies that were equally effective for students with different
needs. The movement took its name and strategy from architects'
response to the need to design public and commercial buildings
that were "handicapped accessible." Architects decided to focus
on designs that not only allowed wheelchairs access to buildings,
but also accommodated the broadest set of needs that people
have—such as mothers with strollers or persons whose recent
injuries did not allow them to lift their legs. Thus, the term *universal design* was coined in architecture. Just as a ramp at a building
may serve many different needs of individuals, there are a number
of instructional strategies that are equally helpful to students with
different learning challenges.

As the enthusiasm for a universal design for learning grew,
however, many groups crowded under the umbrella. While the
concept still refers to developing a curriculum that is sufficiently
flexible to serve a diverse set of needs, something has been lost in
the translation. Commercial endeavors sell "universal designs"
that address highly specific learning disabilities. The challenge,
unfortunately, to develop a flexible curriculum that, like the ramp
at public buildings, serves a variety of needs lies largely ahead of
us. That said, the central message of the original research should
not be forgotten: many instructional strategies—such as tactile
experiences and visual illustrations—provide quality support to
the learning needs of English language learners, students with
some learning disabilities, and even marginal students with no
defined disabilities.

Tutoring support systems: One-on-one tutoring is not only part of
the new RTI process, but also a common method schools have
used to support struggling students for at least the last 50 years.
Community volunteers, providers of supplementary education
services, and even students themselves serve as tutors in our

nation's public schools. The challenge has been, and remains, how to ensure that the activities of the tutor address the specific needs of the tutee. Interim assessments and electronic technology will continue to reduce the challenge of aligning tutoring activities with specific student needs.

Research increasingly demonstrates, though, that using experienced teachers as tutors has the greatest likelihood of generating sustainable improvements for struggling students (Gordon, 2009), assuming that teachers rely on structured programs and frequent diagnostics. Finland, a nation with some of the world's highest achieving students, has specially trained tutors in all its schools. Typically, one tutor serves students from seven classrooms. Struggling students are promptly provided tutoring to help them catch up with their regular class. Approximately 30 percent of Finnish students receive tutoring during a given year (Gordon, 2009).

Substantial gains in student learning have also been realized with peer tutoring. Perhaps best known is the program, Peer Assisted Learning (PALS), developed by Doug and Lynn Fuchs. It provides structured activities and questioning, and, over time, students serve both as tutor and tutee (Fuchs, Fuchs, & Burish, 2000).

Peer tutoring, in general, has some distinct advantages: students get quick feedback, are more actively engaged, increase their abilities to reflect on their learning, and demonstrate an increased ability to apply what they are learning to new situations (Greenwood, Carta, & Kamps, 1990). Some cautionary advice from those who have adopted peer tutoring strategies includes understanding that not all students will be equally motivated, students will need specific training in how to provide feedback, and teachers will need to monitor tutoring sessions to ensure that students maintain fidelity to the protocol and interest in the other students' success (Foorman & Torgeson, 2001).

CONCLUSION

In this chapter, we identified ways in which curriculum alignment can remain a problem, even in this era of state standards and district pacing guides; ways in which teachers' collaboration across grades and subjects can provide new opportunities to help struggling students; ways in which schools will be expected to help prevent the incidence of disabilities in later grades through early intervention; and ways in which coteaching partnerships can make complex subjects accessible to marginal or struggling students. We also sought to emphasize the value of health-related curriculum and activities in meeting academic goals.

CHAPTER TEN

Technology

Predicting future advances of education technology is no easy task. In 1999, students enrolled in an education technology class at University of Illinois created an innovation timeline that included the following:

- 2005: Students' electronic notebooks would have the first interactive textbook
- 2024: Most schooling activities will occur at home
- 2084: Students will be taught by robots (Bruce, 2001)

The anticipation of robot teachers, clearly, is the most curious prediction. Perhaps students envisioned the patient voice on most of our GPS systems ("recalculating route") would be available as they worked through complex mathematical problems.

The use of technology in educational settings has not been without critics. While students were envisioning the future of education technology, Stanford education professor Larry Cuban (2001) was concluding that the benefits of new technologies in schools failed to match the nation's investment. Most evaluators in the late 1990s and early 2000s, such as Cuban, focused on instructional technologies which, in retrospect were quite primitive: software helped students with basic skills but had lacked the capacity to adapt to an individual student's proficiency level, or online learning often helped students acquire college credits but without an engaging interactive capacity. Yet, the technology revolution in education during the first decade of this century involved communication and managerial challenges. This is not surprising.

Clayton Christensen and his colleagues (2008)—experts in the innovation process at large corporations—find that large success-ful corporations (and school districts) easily adopt technologies allowing them to improve those things that they are already doing. For schools and school districts, this generally includes communi-cation and productivity functions. For instance, teacher portals that allow them to access class materials and grades, anywhere, anytime, adds convenience in completing a task.

On the other hand, the study predicts that new technologies requiring changes in instructional strategies will have low adop-tion rates. Christensen and colleagues argue that technologies requiring major changes in "how we do business" emerge not in well-established institutions like public school systems, but rather in newly formed institutions of learning. A recent study (Picciano & Seaman, 2009) finds district curriculum directors' assessment follows Christensen's argument: if the new technology requires a number of changes in instructional practices or considerable investment in time learning to use it, then it won't be adopted. Substantive changes in how learning is organized will occur, instead, on the edges—in courses that were previously unavailable in the school district, such as some Advanced Placement or credit recovery programs (Christensen et al., 2008).

We think this pessimism is misplaced. Ignored by the critics and forecasters alike was the degree to which technologies for communication and productivity allowed educators not only to improve what they were already doing, but to increase their ability to be responsive to students and parents. Electronic communica-tion systems greatly increased professional collaboration among educators and, at last, are providing more and more parents with "real time" access to their child's attendance and performance records. Attempting any measurement of the impact of these alternative applications of technology is impossible, but the trans-formation should not go unnoticed. The Technology Action Team should take measure of the challenge. If schools or districts lack technology that enhances communication and productivity, then the acquisition of such should be the first priority.

While technology can and should be understood as any electronic tool used to complete a task, our focus will be primarily on those electronically based tools that enhance the quality of instruction, improve communication, or increase productivity. In this chapter, we focus on using technology to increase productivity and professional practice, improve teaching and learning, and identify ways in which students' opportunities to learn reflect emerging national standards in technology.

A strong Technology Action Team includes both learners and "geeks." The learners keep the computer geeks on the ground, and serve as "reality tests" for not only the ways in which technology-novice teachers can acquire fluency with new technologies, but also initial indicators of what low-tech teachers may perceive as needs. The technology geeks keep their colleagues abreast of new opportunities—in terms of improving both the learning opportunities of students as well as those of teachers.

The Technology Action Team is part of the front guard in identifying ways in which the school's *existing* technology resources can be adapted or redirected to support student learning. Given the investment needed by educators to become effective users of technology in classroom instruction, we recommend that the action team first ensure that educators have the skills and resources to use those technologies related to communication and productivity. If those are fully utilized in the school, then the focus on instructional technology is a first priority.

The action team also develops strategies for supporting educators as they master new instructional and productivity-related technology. Finally, the action team ensures that educators are familiar with their existing state technology standards for students, and, as appropriate, helps school staff develop opportunities for students to master these standards. When schools have options in acquiring new technologies, the team should be able to provide some assessment of the relative value of one technology over another in advancing school goals. The particulars of these responsibilities necessarily will vary from school to school.

IDENTIFYING AVAILABLE TECHNOLOGY AND ITS USE

The most sensible first step, regardless of the particulars, for any Technology Action Team is to inventory fellow educators' current use of newer technologies available to teachers. This includes those designed to support student learning, improve communication with parents, or provide or enhance professional development. Table 10.1 provides the action team with some guidance in developing their inventory.

Having an accurate picture of what's available and how educators are using it is the only way to sensibly take the first steps with an action plan. Many districts provide software that allows educators to provide their course outline and assignments. Some even have private parent portals that allow them to access student class records. That said, teachers vary widely in their use of available technology both within and across schools.

If technology resources appear to be underutilized, the Technology Action Team should identify the weaknesses in the needed support system available to teachers. Figure 10.1 illustrates the critical aspects of a support system for using technology.

Table 10.1   Technology Team Inventory: What's Here and How Are We Using It?

- Distribution of hardware for student use—classes, labs, study hall?
- Dedicated computer and printer for teachers? In each classroom?
- Locations of Internet access?
- Internet use in classroom?
  1. Development of lesson plans.
  2. Teacher presentations or demonstrations.
  3. Student assignments.
  4. Student tutorials.
  5. Communication.
  6. Online professional development.

- Availability and use of instructional management system?
  1. Attendance and grades.
  2. Lesson plans and student assignments.
  3. Student portfolios.
  4. Instructional resources.
  5. Capacity to share lesson plans and student activities.
  6. Availability of tutorial remedial software.

- Other technology: distribution and use?
  1. Whiteboards.
  2. Clickers.
  3. Media equipment—sound, video, and other broadcasting equipment.
  4. Media library.
  5. Assistive technology.

Figure 10.1   Conditions Needed for Teachers to Use Technology

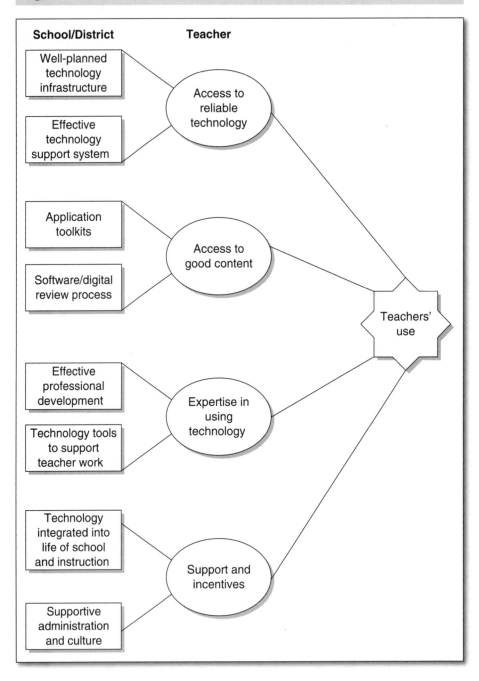

IMPROVING PROFESSIONAL PRACTICE

The possibilities for improving professional practice with technology are not just a function of new hardware needed but also the imaginative spirit of those using them. Young teachers, for instance, see new opportunities to reduce the burden of daily routines; they may use "tablet" technology to take attendance, give lunch projections and preferences, and report grades.

Improving educators' productivity and professional practice through technology generally refers to software (and the appropriate hardware) that reduces the amount of time teachers must devote to maintaining records, increases their ability to individualize (or differentiate) instruction in a more timely fashion, expands their options in designing instruction, or improves the frequency or quality of communication among members of the school community.

Perhaps one of the most interesting opportunities for educators to enhance professional practice lies with the ability to increase communication and thus collaboration with parents. It can be as personal as voice mail left by a teacher on the parent's cell phone or as impersonal as a letter generated electronically that notifies parents when their children are receiving failing grades in one or more of their classes. Parent portals allow parents electronic access to their children's current information on attendance, grades, class schedules, disciplinary or counseling reports, and current assignments and due dates.

Instructional management systems with an open architecture remain one of the more underutilized tools for improving productivity. While the capacity of each system differs, a fully integrated system should have not only methods for maintaining classroom records on each student, but also the capacity to maintain and share lesson plans and student work. Students and parents may have access to their portfolios, future assignments, attendance, and grades. Of course, students could actually complete their assignments online and store them in a portfolio file. Teachers may share classroom activities and provide commentary on the types of students especially responsive to each activity. Many companies offer management systems that provide some of these capabilities, but few offer a system that links the data with resources that teachers routinely use or need. Such portfolios serve as excellent data for professional learning communities to assess the relative effectiveness of assignments that focus on a given concept. Response to Intervention Teams may use the portfolio data to gain a different perspective on struggling students. When it comes to recommending tools for improving professional practice, a Technology Action Team best serves a school when it focuses on the dictum: technology works best in response to a perceived need or weakness (Simpson & Oliver, 2007).

New technologies also provide new forums for improving professional practice. Early efforts at such were characterized by talking heads, blackboards, and flip charts sent out to distant places where teachers sat dutifully in an auditorium or classroom to hear about new approaches to instructional practice. Often, the only measure of success was sitting there long enough to be considered in attendance. With that history, it's not hard to understand why teachers often consider online professional development courses less rigorous than extended workshops.

Times are changing. The flexibility and interactivity of more recent online professional development available to teachers require much more engagement and responsibility. Referred to as a facilitated format, new forms of e-learning for teachers work from a platform that expects teachers to not just listen, but to implement specific strategies and reflect upon them in the company of colleagues and an expert. Teachers may access readings on a new instructional approach at their convenience, complete some assignments (perhaps piloting a new strategy), and then discuss the assignments and readings with other teachers—maybe focusing on what did or did not work as they attempted to implement the new strategy. The new professional development series sponsored by PBS and many new state resources rely exclusively on the facilitated format.

Facilitated formats for professional development may have some advantages. Harvard professor Christopher Dede says:

> It's pretty hard to stand up face to face in front of a group of your peers and admit you're not as great of a teacher as you could be. Most people find being online disinhibiting a little bit. That kind of dialogue is important. Professional development can't really start with the idea that you're perfect. (as cited in Sawchuck, 2009, p. 23)

While opportunities for educators to engage in professional development opportunities online increases almost daily, the quality remains uneven. Several organizations, including the National Education Association, help educators identify high-quality sessions using a peer-review process.

Many national experts, though, continue to be concerned about the degree to which online professional development could undermine the increasingly meaningful development of professional learning communities at each school. In an interview with *Education Week* (Sawchuck, 2009), Joellen Killion, an executive at Learning Forward (formerly known as the National Staff Development Council), said:

> One of the things we've been nervous about with online learning is that it could set us back decades where districts purchase access to a series of online courses for teachers, and teachers go home at night and sit alone in front of their computers, answering questions all in isolation. (p. 24)

Professional support groups relying on Twitter are increasingly common, especially among young people new to the profession. A small problem reported on Twitter can quickly generate some ideas in a timely way. Educators usually form groups around a specific course, but a variety of interest groups can be found through Twitter.

Many, if not most, of the efforts of the Technology Action Team will be done in collaboration with other action teams. In adopting new technologies, these questions should always be addressed: What problems are we trying to solve? Is the effort required to gain fluency with the technology balanced by the advantages educators will gain? What are the simple and predictable problems that teachers will encounter as they attempt to gain fluency with the technology? What type of training and support will minimize the predictable frustrations novices will encounter?

IMPROVING THE QUALITY OF TEACHING AND LEARNING

While robot teachers may not be on the horizon, the availability of interactive and adaptive technologies greatly increases the likelihood that technology will be used not only to improve our ability to address the needs of diverse learners, but also to challenge all students intellectually. Interactive technologies are those that require the learner to respond—contrasted with those that are limited to listening or viewing. Adaptive technologies are those with queries that vary depending on the previous responses of students.

Rigorous studies of effectiveness of various instructional technologies are only beginning to emerge. Recent British studies illustrate the central challenge. Attempting to assess the value of interactive whiteboards, researchers found different results. (Whiteboards are electronic display devices that not only replace flip charts and blackboards but also link to a computer and projector. Users may display materials from the Internet or local systems and notes can be made on the whiteboard and captured permanently for other uses.)

In one study, interactive whiteboards were introduced into 97 elementary schools and those schools matched with others continuing with their usual resources. After the end of the first year, researchers concluded that whiteboards "slowed the pace of instruction" and resulted in "overvaluing the most mundane activities" and were more cumbersome than previous technologies (British Broadcasting Company, 2007).

On the other hand, a study of those same teachers' use for two years of the interactive whiteboards found some significant achievement gains for those students enrolled in the 97 classes where teachers relied upon the interactive boards versus those who did not (Somekh, 2007). Learning gains for over 7,000 students were matched against standard gains in mathematics, science, and reading. Significantly greater gains were observed in classrooms with interactive whiteboards, especially with girls in mathematics and science.

The contrasting results confirm what others are finding in studies in the United States: it takes about two years for teachers to "change the way we do business" in ways that can actually make a difference in student learning. Marzano's (2009) study of interactive whiteboards confirms that finding and adds further specification: the greatest effect of whiteboard technology on student learning occurs when teachers use them at least 40 percent of the time but less than 80 percent, and when teachers have high confidence in their ability to use the technology.

In fact, the learning curve for many new instructional technologies is unclear. Some of the most powerful tools require substantial changes in instructional strategies—to say nothing of the technical support that teachers may need to become fluent in their use. Interactive technologies appear to have their greatest effect on student learning via their effect on engagement and motivation (Metiri Group, 2006).

Successfully using new technological resources as learning tools requires more than access to the resources and trained instructors. It also requires that educators reflect critically on the capacity of the tools to deliver the type of learning that fits with specific educational needs.

Researchers evaluate the usefulness of instructional technologies in terms of their potential to improve students' capacity to do one or more of the following:

- *Develop fluency with facts and basic knowledge:* Will students' ability to complete tasks and recall facts with automaticity increase with the use of this tool?
- *Create a conceptual framework or deepen students' expertise in a content area:* Will students increase their understanding of one or more concepts in ways that allow them to apply it to new and novel situations?
- *Process and visualize information:* Does the technology improve students' ability to interpret, evaluate, and use multimedia-based information in ways that advance thinking or decision making?
- *Engage in higher-order thinking:* Does the technology improve students' ability to analyze or compare alternatives in subject-based problem-solving activities?
- *Perceive relevancy:* Does the technology help students understand the application of concepts to challenging, real-world problems? (Adapted from Metiri Group, 2006)

We frame our discussion of instructional technology from the perspective of a teacher: teachers can use technology to develop or enrich the instructional activities they design, to supplement classroom instruction, or to replace classroom instruction entirely. We identify those types of educational needs that the tools can address and, where possible, provide research evidence on their efficacy.

Enriching instructional activities: When teachers use technology to enrich or develop instruction, they are active, creative agents in designing the learning experience. They may incorporate "raw" Internet-based resources to enrich an existing activity, develop a framework for student inquiry, or create an actual textbook using software associated with Wikipedia.

To acknowledge the wealth of information and artifacts available as "raw" resources on the Internet is to state the obvious. The Library of Congress's rich online collection, American Memory, electronically houses artifacts of American life, with collections of advertising and art as well as film and audio recordings of civic ceremonies or folk life. The National Archives' online resources allow access to census, military, and immigration records as well as historical documents. Then, of course, there's a dizzying array of labor statistics, population charts and graphs, and pictures from space only a few clicks away.

Such resources provide educators with exceptional opportunities to help students perceive the relevancy of a given topic or concept. By establishing a framework for inquiry, educators may allow students to organize such raw data and—with the right questions—engage students in higher-order thinking or problem solving. For some subjects, such as science, educators have an abundance of information they can use to deepen students' understanding of basic concepts. The challenge, of course, is the investment of time required to incorporate such resources in meaningful and engaging ways.

Developing activities or courses: It is one thing to enrich existing instructional activities with so-called raw resources found on the Internet; it's another to develop entirely new courses or activities with them. Online tools, such as Wiki, provide opportunities for teachers to collaborate across subjects within a school as well as across schools within the same subject. Teachers may collaborate to create lesson plans, track the progress of implementation, and share portfolios of student work. Teachers have even attempted to develop collaborative textbooks with such tools, although most evidence suggests that such projects have rarely been completed.

Students Using Technology to Assist Teachers

Students at a rural Texas high school have developed lessons about the local cotton production industry, which they are sharing with younger students in other parts of the country through videoconferencing technology. The Texas students researched and developed their lesson, which they aligned with national standards for Grades 3–5 geography, history, and science; filmed a video for the presentation; and created classroom materials for remote teachers to distribute to students ahead of time.

Source: Harrison, 2010.

In these creative efforts, incorporating tools such as an interactive whiteboard may improve students' capacity to create a conceptual framework and process and visualize multimedia information. Increasingly frequent companions to interactive whiteboards are classroom response systems (sometimes referred to as *clickers*) that allow students to respond individually to teacher queries. Teachers have used them to gain some formative assessment or to increase student engagement. Most of the research on classroom response systems has been done at the postsecondary level with large lecture classes. While the initial responses of students will vary from great enthusiasm to revulsion, some evidence shows that learning improved with such response systems as the novelty wore off (Simpson & Oliver, 2007); that is, students were less distracted by the novelty of the tool and focused on the questions asked by the teachers.

Lest educators become too complacent about developing opportunities for students to develop Internet investigative skills, future assessments will assume that students already have such skills. A recent study of assessments in technology-rich environments (TREs) illustrates the types of problems students may encounter:

The search scenario required students to locate and synthesize scientific information about helium balloons from a simulated World Wide Web environment. The TRE simulation scenario required students to experiment to solve problems of increasing complexity about relationships among buoyancy, mass, and volume; students viewed animated displays after manipulating the mass carried by a scientific helium balloon and the amount of helium contained in the balloon. Both scenarios targeted Grade 8 students who were assumed to have basic computer skills; basic exposure to scientific inquiry and concepts of buoyancy, mass, and volume; and the ability to read scientifically oriented material at a sixth-grade level or higher. (Bennett et al., 2007)

Educators may find increasing opportunities to develop or adapt investigative activities such as these. They may well prove to be one of the more potent learning experiences we can provide students.

Supplemental resources: Supplemental resources refer to classroom-ready activities or lesson plans available in a variety of mediums. Supplemental resources, mostly available on the Internet, provide educators the opportunity to build upon the work of others. Even classroom-ready activities will usually require some adaptation to fit the prior understandings of the students in a teacher's class. Here, we discuss public-use lesson plans available from federal and state agencies and online teacher communities as well as services that allow teachers to publicly address the needs of struggling students.

- *Publicly available lesson plans:* Online teacher communities, such as those on TeachNet, have classroom-ready activities organized by subject and grade level, often with some commentary from teachers about how they used the material and what rating they would give it. National Aeronautics and Space Administration (NASA) also provides a number of classroom-ready activities. The Technology Action Team may wish to identify websites that provide lesson plans or activities that may help educators address specific academic needs.

- *Computer assisted instruction:* Numerous software programs, many linked to various textbook series, give students opportunities to increase their fluency in mathematics or reading. Schools make extensive use of these programs to assist struggling students, and studies support some advantages over traditional strategies (Metiri Group, 2006). The technical and scientific sophistication of these support systems are increasing and should have greater capacity to improve students' conceptual understanding and make adaptations to the various needs of struggling students.

• *Online textbooks:* California recently endorsed 10 math and science digital textbooks for high school courses. The free digital textbooks will help districts save money and create more interactive environments for student learning (Chea, 2009). However, the promise of not only cheaper textbooks, but better ones, introduces new problems. Educators in California now confront the issue of how to provide access to the materials when insufficient computers are available at school and some students lack Internet access at home.

The introduction of digital textbooks suggests that the national goal of having 1:1 ratio of students to computers may need to be reassessed. As of 2008, 3.8 students, on average, share one instructional computer (Technology Counts, 2009). The possibility of digital textbooks adds even more complexity to the long held goal of one computer for every student: Should students have 24-hour access or only in-school access to computers? Should the student or the school own the equipment? Which of the various hardware options should be considered—notebooks, tablets, and/or wireless reading devices? Ironically, the issue of equity likely will become more challenging as technological inventions proliferate.

When and if a school faces the dilemma of relying upon instructional technologies that create potential inequities, the Technology Action Team may collaborate with the Family and Community Partnerships Action Team to identify strategies that reduce, or preferably eliminate, possible inequities.

• *Replacing classroom instruction:* Competing with teacher created or managed technologies designed to enhance student learning are those prepackaged (or self-contained) instructional technologies—best known as e-learning or virtual classes. These usually require teachers to possess few, if any, technology skills and certainly little development time.

E-learning, or virtual classes for students, is increasingly common. The Sloan Consortium's report (as cited in Picciano & Seaman, 2009) estimates that in 2008–09 over one million students relied upon these courses—a 48 percent increase since 2007.

While e-learning serves both advanced students as well as those struggling to reach grade level in a given subject area, industry experts find that more students are using e-learning for credit recovery than for Advanced Placement courses (Watson, Gemin, & Ryan, 2008). Smaller districts report using e-learning as a way to differentiate instruction. They use multiple online courses, for instance, in science, in one classroom to increase the likelihood that all students have challenging learning experiences. Blended courses—including both online and teacher-led instruction—are the most popular ways in which to incorporate online materials (Davis, 2009).

Research findings suggest that students are performing as well in these learning environments as traditional ones (Metiri Group, 2006). The only exception appears to be those learning activities delivered via videoconferencing: evidence suggests that it is not as effective as traditional environments.

Anticipating greater use of online courses in postsecondary education, the state of Michigan now includes an "online learning experience" as part of its high school graduation requirements.

EMERGING TECHNOLOGY STANDARDS FOR STUDENTS

Existing national technology standards for students focus largely on the utilization of technology—what students should know and be able to do with various software and Internet resources. The initial framework for assessing students' technological literacy (through the National Assessment of Education Progress [NAEP]) expands the scope to include all types of technology and its implications for social issues, such as the ethical issues related to privacy and the effects of technology on societies.

The International Society for Technology in Education (ISTE) provides technology standards for teachers, administrators, and students. The 2007 edition of the students' standards includes six core areas: creativity and innovation; communication and collaboration; research information and fluency; critical thinking, problem solving, and decision making; digital citizenship; and technology operations and concepts.

1. *Creativity and innovation:* Students use technology to model or simulate complex issues or systems, apply what they know to generate new approaches to problems, and identify trends and make forecasts.

2. *Communication and collaboration:* Students know how to use digital media to communicate and collaborate with others—developing products online in collaboration with others.

3. *Research and information fluency:* Students know how to retrieve information from a variety of sources, evaluate its usefulness and authoritative value, and synthesize and organize the information.

4. *Critical thinking, problem solving, and decision making:* Students know how to plan investigations and make decisions about the appropriate tools and resources they will need to effectively address the central questions of the investigation.

5. *Digital citizenship:* Students demonstrate a commitment to responsible use of technology and understand the safe and legal uses of it.

6. *Technology operations and concepts:* Students demonstrate a sound understanding of technology concepts, systems, and operations as evidenced by their ability to troubleshoot and transfer what they know to new technologies (ISTE, 2007).

Each state adapted these national technology standards to meet the needs they anticipate for their students. Some include additional skills; others expand the concept of technology literacy to include the dilemmas that new technologies introduce, such as privacy and energy consumption.

Renewed interest in what we should expect students to know about technology and be able to do with "it" will become an increasingly important debate among policymakers and educators in the coming years. The NAEP—with board membership that includes governors, scholars, and educators—will be setting the stage for new discussions and debates about what students will need to know as citizens and successful participants in our nation's economy.

In 2012, the first national assessment of technology literacy will be administered. The preliminary framework for only assessment embraces a broad view of technology—not only computer systems and their related software, but all technologies—such as those associated with transportation, domestic activities, and social networks. Students, according to the proposed NAEP framework for technological literacy, should acquire not only the skills and knowledge associated with new technologies, but also understand the dilemmas that new technologies introduce to society as well as the design and systems that undergird them. This proposed framework for technology literacy has broad implications for K–12 education. At minimum, science and engineering will become an integral component of technological literacy.

CONCLUSION

If future applications of technology in K–12 schooling follow the path predicted by industry innovation experts such as Clayton Christensen, we may expect the future applications of technology to look something like this: If it makes what we already do better, we will adopt it. If it requires changing the way we do things, it will be ignored.

If that prediction holds for American public education, then we can expect districts and schools to invest most heavily in new productivity tools. E-learning systems will become increasingly common for Advanced Placement courses, credit recovery, and professional development. Computer-assisted instruction will become the treatment of choice for remediation. Class schedules, lessons, and assignments will continue to look much the same.

What innovation experts fail to take into account, however, is the possible transformational push brought on with the arrival of "tech generation" teachers, that is, the generation of young people who don't recall a time that they were not texting or Twittering friends, manipulating electronic files, or playing electronic games. Their technological fluency should reduce the time educators need to invest in learning how to use, for example, an interactive whiteboard.

A Technology Action Team needs a plan for incorporating learning tools. The first step in any plan is to know what technologies are available, which are being used, by whom, and to what effect. The inventory should include not only instructional tools, but also those related to productivity and communication. A second step is to gain an understanding, most often from other action teams, of needs that are not being met.

Some questions to answer when considering the adoption of a new technology include: What problems are we trying to solve? Is the effort required to gain fluency with the technology balanced by the advantages educators will gain? How do we minimize the operational frustrations during the learning phase? What are the simple and predictable problems that teachers will encounter as they attempt to gain fluency with the technology?

When it comes to productivity and communication tools, a Technology Action Team best serves a school when it focuses on the dictum: technology works best in response to a specific weakness or need (Simpson & Oliver, 2007). Building a castle in which no one wants to live can be frustrating.

C H A P T E R   E L E V E N

Professional Development

Professional development remains one of the key ingredients in helping educators improve student learning at their schools. In fact, some of the best studies of professional development suggest that teachers receiving an average of 49 hours can boost their students' achievement by 23 percentile points (Yoon, Duncan, Lee, Scarloss, & Shapley, 2007). Even though teachers, in a 2005 national survey, reported an average of 66 hours of professional development during the 2003–04 school year (Birman et al., 2007), we've yet to see the striking results anticipated by some researchers. The issues in professional development, we believe, are not so much about the time available for professional development, but how that time is used.

Mary Kennedy's (1998) early synthesis of research findings on effective professional development programs remain fairly robust today: "Programs whose content focused mainly on teachers' behaviors demonstrated smaller influences on student learning than did programs whose focus on teachers' knowledge of the subject, on the curriculum, or on how students learn the subject" (p. 19). While teachers in 2004 devoted much more time to professional development than in the 1990s, studies find that less than half of the time focuses on deeper analysis of subject area issues or challenges in student learning in those subjects (Birman et al., 2007).

Therefore, one barrier to realizing the benefits of professional development is the lack of opportunity for teachers to dig deeply into a subject area and improve their understanding of the typical challenges students encounter. Over and above the focus on content, researchers find the greatest impact of professional development occurs at schools with strong professional learning communities that include active engagement of teachers, feedback from colleagues, and collaborative reviews of student work (Ingvarson, Meiers, & Beavis, 2005).

Realizing a return on professional development, then, requires that schools be active agents in the process, and where teachers

- discuss teaching and learning issues with each other;
- collaborate in planning, teaching, and assessment activities; and
- share with their colleagues what they have learned in specialized programs.

The Professional Development Action Team serves an essential role in helping school leaders ensure that these school-based supports for professional development become embedded into the everyday life of the school. The team supports other action teams in the school by helping define, organize, and evaluate professional development needs.

Occasionally, Professional Development Action Teams worry that they must provide and present all the professional development for the school. That is not the case. The team should view itself as a resource to other action teams seeking to enhance the capacity of school staff in some area, an advisor to the guiding coalition on effective professional development, a coordinator of various school-wide professional development initiatives, and a strategist for developing and implementing an orientation process for new teachers.

ESTABLISHING RESOURCES AND NEEDS

The Professional Development Action Team should acquire a complete picture of what type of professional development is available and what teachers are doing. While a survey may not be necessary, a systematic inventory is needed. Table 11.1 provides a list of possible sources of professional development. If the team's district has a professional development center that provides centralized workshops or online courses, the team should maintain current listings of these resources.

Second, the Professional Development Action Team should inventory staff regarding their perceived needs. Close coordination with all action teams will be important. The Technology and Data Analysis Action Teams will be essential—both in terms of the content of such an inventory and in terms of collecting any data. Much electronic survey software is available at little cost and will minimize the time any one team will need to devote to the task. Table 11.2 provides an initial overview of the types of professional development that educators may wish or need to pursue.

Whether as individuals, or as a school, educators need to be clear about their goals for improving their skills and knowledge before they develop professional development strategies. It is not uncommon for both individual and collective professional development plans to spin in a separate universe from school improvement goals. The "sit and git" era of professional development understandably drew teachers into workshops where trainers were entertaining or motivational, but attendees lacked a clear sense of

Table 11.1   Where to Look for Professional Development Opportunities

- *Professional learning communities* that meet regularly, in face-to-face meetings, to analyze student work or review student performance issues.
- *District professional development centers,* which have scheduled workshops aligned with school improvement needs.
- *School-based mentoring or coaching* in a one-on-one situation, usually in the classroom.
- *State-sponsored online courses,* which are increasingly interactive and emphasize application and reflection.
- *Internship activities* providing concentrated collaboration with professionals in a lab or industrial setting associated with subject area.
- *Out-of-district conferences* provided by professional organizations, regional centers, the state department of education, etc.
- *Teacher collaboratives or networks* connecting teachers regionally, statewide, nationally, or internationally.
- *Courses for college credit.*
- *National or state workshops and institutes* focusing on a specific topic often supported by state departments of education.

Source: South Dakota Department of Education, 1999.

Table 11.2   Professional Development Topics

- Conceptual foundations of relevant academic subjects
- Effective instructional strategies for diverse learners
- Classroom management skills
- Effective feedback strategies for students
- Working with limited English proficiency students
- Instruction for students with special needs
- Use of technology in communication
- Use of technology for instructional management
- Effective use of technology in classroom instruction
- Using student assessment data to inform instruction
- Improving collaboration with parents

how such experiences were part of a larger effort to advance their professional expertise. Although teachers enjoyed those sessions and were inspired, the learning rarely translated into classroom practice that had an impact on schoolwide improvements. At best, the strategies learned were implemented in isolated classrooms with limited effects on students. At its worse, the workshop provided a modest respite from a tightly scheduled school day.

Yet, it doesn't take years of research to conclude that professional development related to each school's improvement goals has a higher probability of actually making a difference in practice and results. The most effective professional development sessions target the needs of a particular school, grade level, or department. Aligning professional development goals creates a synergy among school teams as they bring different perspectives to a common challenge.

Even the professional development choices of one educator can align with school goals. If the school is challenged by the instructional needs of students with limited proficiency in English, a science teacher may find district workshops or online courses to provide instructional strategies that are especially useful to those students' needs. The Professional Development Action Team should encourage such coordination by identifying and publishing district or state professional development opportunities aligned with school goals.

DEVELOPING AND SUPPORTING SCHOOL-BASED PROFESSIONAL DEVELOPMENT

The Professional Development Action Team is responsible for organizing and keeping track of school-based professional development. The team assists in identifying what skills and time are required for successfully implementing the plan. Sharing individual professional development experiences with colleagues is one form of school-based professional development. For instance, if teachers from several content areas have had the opportunity to attend district or state workshops on improving students' metacognitive skills in particular disciplines, a faculty meeting could be devoted to sharing what they learned and identifying the intersections across subjects.

Induction of new staff members: Within the first five years of teaching, nearly 50 percent of new teachers will leave the profession (American Association of State Colleges and Universities [AASCU], 2006). Continuing with current practices for supporting new teachers, it can take years to develop effective skills in classroom instruction and classroom management. In one study (Public Agenda & NCCTQ, 2007) about on-the-job support, 54 percent of new alternative route teachers said lack of support from administrators was a major drawback to teaching in high-needs schools. Regardless of district support, their route to certification or prior teaching experience needs some orientation to their new school—from its academic strengths and weaknesses to the best place to grab some coffee on the way to work.

Not withstanding district support systems for newly hired teachers, new teachers will need extra support acquainting them with standard practices that may be unique to the school, introducing them to the background and culture of student populations. The Professional Development Action Team should review existing practices at the school as well as districtwide services for new teachers to identify gaps in their orientation and induction. Once the unmet needs of new teachers are identified, the Professional Development Action Team may recommend special school orientation sessions, mentoring responsibilities for some staff, or additional resource materials.

Professional learning communities: Kathleen Cushman (1996) illustrated the potential impact of professional learning communities with this story:

> The *New York Times* science pages told the story of the heart surgeons in Maine, New Hampshire, and Vermont—there are only 23 in all—who agreed in 1993 to observe each other regularly in the operating room and share their know-how, insights, and approaches. In the two years after their nine-month-long project, the death rate among their patients fell by an astonishing 25 percent. Merely by emphasizing teamwork and communication instead of functioning like solitary craftsmen, the study showed, all the doctors brought about major changes in their individual and institutional practices. For teachers who, like heart surgeons, have traditionally worked as isolated professionals, the experiment holds a powerful lesson. If their goal is to lower the "death rate" of young minds and see them thrive, many educators now emphatically believe, they can do it better together than by working alone. (p. 5)

Over the last 20 years, professional learning communities have evolved from forums for sharing ideas to effective forms of professional development in which teachers learn by working together with a sharp focus on using data and research to determine effective teacher practices and the effect on student learning. Ongoing professional development strategies that extend over time and engage teachers in continuous efforts to improve their craft consistently show greater effectiveness than other methods.

Schools can have several tiers of professional learning communities. They may be organized through grade-level teams, departments, or multiage house teams. Teams that share the same students serve different purposes than teams that share the same subject area. In our experience, each type serves unique and important purposes and opportunities for collaboration, so both types should be considered. When asked to help an Illinois middle school devise a training program for analyzing student work, we began with a team made up of members from each of the subject areas—anticipating that this would allow them to transfer their expertise to their respective departments. We were surprised at the strategy the teachers chose for going to scale: they decided that the interdepartmental membership of the group was an essential component of the learning experience. Schools differ, then, in their immediate needs, but over time the professional learning communities should vary.

Approaches

Looking at student work: The practice of looking at student work emerged at an international conference of teachers in the 1990s when they were assigned the task of framing standards for high-quality instruction. Using assignments developed by teachers and the resulting student work as evidence, they sought to see what types of assignments generated meaningful results in terms of student learning.

> "Students can do no better than the assignments they are given."
>
> Collaborative Communications Group, Edna McConnell Clark Foundation, 2002

By the second day of their efforts, teachers commented that the discussions of student work were the most meaningful professional experiences they had ever had. Since that time, protocols for looking at student work have flourished and many schools across the country have sought to use them.

Protocols for looking at student work almost universally require the following:

- specific time allocations for different tasks or discussions;
- limiting the number of participating teachers from 8 to 12;
- discussing an assignment and student work from one of the participating teachers; and
- norms that result in constructive, nonjudgmental discussions.

Protocols differ in terms of the following:

- the link they establish with state standards,
- the emphasis they give to the assignment relative to a student's work,
- what information is provided about the student,

- the degree to which they assess the evidence for what students understand, and
- whether or not they consider how the assignment might be changed to improve the outcome.

The website Looking At Student Work (LASW), sponsored by the Annenberg Institute for School Reform, provides a number of links to protocols, many of which are specific to grade levels; others are specific to content areas.

Creating trust among the participants and establishing an agenda with time allocations are essential ingredients. Teachers are often surprised by the variety of conversations that emerge—perhaps it's exploring the meaning of certain concepts in their subject area, how some educators address predictable misconceptions held by students, or the serendipitous opportunities to make connections across subject areas.

Collaboration will occur in a variety of ways. For instance, if the goal is to improve students' writing skills in the content areas, this team would work with the Curriculum and Instruction Action Team for ways in which they could profile needs in that area—through self-assessment surveys, established rubrics, or perhaps departmental or grade-level team discussions.

The Professional Development Action Team should help school leaders think creatively about the opportunities. We find many schools are able to squeeze planned opportunities for professional learning into existing schedules using the following:

- staff meetings,
- department meetings,
- grade-level meetings,
- early release days, or
- release time provided by a substitute for one or two class periods per month.

In developing options for professional development that will address schoolwide improvement goals, it is important to avoid tactics that emphasize quick fixes for student test scores—with a new "tidbit" every week. Instead, the plan should focus on long-term, systematic investments that build a particular capacity. For instance, professional learning communities may follow an iterative process analyzing students' understanding of a particularly difficult concept, identifying alternative strategies, experimenting with them, and reconvening to review the results.

Sharing a goal, differentiating activities: School-level professional development activities also can use different approaches to the same school goal. Teachers at one middle school—where improving reading comprehension was a primary goal in their school improvement plan—committed themselves to teaching reading comprehension strategies across the content areas. Using district rubrics for these strategies, teachers profiled their current practices. Most of the content teachers reported limited proficiency in the recommended practices for their content area. The professional development team presented several options that departments might consider, and these were the results:

- One department formed a book study group to read and discuss a book on a topic highly recommended by the district curriculum director.
- Another department—whose members had attended training on the topic several years ago—chose to meet to review their materials and to reflect on their current practice.
- A few teachers from different departments elected to observe a teacher at the high school with a strong track record in teaching reading comprehension in his social studies classes and subsequently observe each other as they incorporated some of the essential processes.

Teachers agreed to incorporate new strategies for improving reading comprehension and develop assessments to monitor student learning. At the end of the semester, they assessed their current practices using the district rubric and used student work to assess the degree to which the strategies had some effect on student learning. The self-assessments and analysis of student work allowed them to determine what next steps were needed. In this instance, each teacher had choices, but they all were learning about the same topic, were intent on becoming proficient on the district rubric, and collected student data on the impact of their efforts.

Online professional development: Current estimates suggest that about 20 percent of all K–12 professional development is provided online. Christopher Dede, a Harvard professor and leading authority on online professional development, anticipates that its use will continue to grow. It has several advantages over workshops and other forms of training: it can encourage more individual reflection, provide a greater match with individual learning styles, and allow educators to participate at a time convenient for them (Dede, 2006).

Online professional development can also be a collective experience, and thus part of the professional learning community structure. Open education resources (OER) provide educators with access to world-renowned specialists in almost every subject imaginable. Teachers can watch lectures or work in interactive formats at their convenience and then meet to discuss the implications of what they've learned for improving student learning at their school.

Initial research suggests that interactive and reflective online professional development can create equivalent results to workshops and off-site training. The Professional Development Action Team can support such efforts by collaborating with the Technology Action Team to identify online opportunities that teachers may wish to explore.

Milbrey McLaughlin and Joan Talbert (2006) rightly emphasize that school-based learning communities should not replace off-site professional development. In fact, the off-site professional development is essential if the school-based communities are to be effective. In the systems-based model, though, off-site professional development programs should increase the leverage that educators can realize on common organizational goals.

ASSESSING IMPACT AND FUTURE NEEDS

Each professional development workshop or session should have specific expectations identified at the beginning of the session describing the expected outcomes in terms of teacher behavior. Every session should begin with a clear link between the objectives and the need: What current student performance data indicates a need for the session's objectives? Using a rubric before, during, and after a session allows teachers to assess the impact on their knowledge and practice.

Professional development sessions, be they school-based or off-site, should provide time for reflection and planning—either in appropriate groups or individually. In most instances, changes in practice emerge in small increments and it is best to encourage plans to reflect such.

Quick response surveys of teachers several weeks after a professional development session allow the team to identify challenges in implementing plans that could be addressed through coaching or professional learning community meetings. Whatever the strategy, it must reflect the fact that long-term impact of professional development is seldom predicted from an "in the moment" response of participants.

The Professional Development Action Team should collaborate with the Data Analysis Action Team. Periodic feedback, perhaps through interim assessments, will allow all to assess the impact of these efforts. Just as in the classroom, the assessment of implementation and student learning should be an ongoing process that begins at the beginning, that is, at the planning stages.

Evaluating school-based professional development should include indicators of the degree to which educators had the opportunity to

- build their knowledge base,
- observe models of effective practice,
- reflect on how they can incorporate new practices,
- have support and feedback in the adoption of new models, and
- assess the impact of their efforts.

Determining professional development needs is not a one-time activity. It should be an ongoing process that allows for different topics, differing teacher needs, differing levels of support, a variety of models to learn from, and ongoing evaluation of teachers' needs and student achievement tied to teachers' actions. Just as we differentiate our instruction in the classroom, the professional development should be differentiated to help teachers learn what they need to learn in a way that is most effective for them.

CONCLUSION

The Professional Development Action Team is a critical force for creating powerful results. An inventory of professional development opportunities provided by the district or state should serve as a baseline inventory of resources. Given the goals of the school improvement plan, the team can help educators by identifying online opportunities, conferences, or district training that should deepen each educator's capacity to reach schoolwide goals. School-based professional development should include an induction program for new teachers in the school and professional learning communities. The team supports and guides professional learning communities by helping them create a process for analyzing student work, collaborating on lessons, and observing each other.

The team should ensure that all teachers participate in assessing the value of school-based professional development and make recommendations for future work that reflects both those evaluations and emerging needs.

Collaboration with other action teams likely should occur often. The Professional Development Action Team may recommend professional development strategies to address the priorities of the Curriculum and Instruction Action Team. The Data Analysis Action Team may help the Professional Development Action Team monitor the impact of the professional learning communities or specific professional development sessions. Professional development activities should always seek to increase teachers' capacity for continuous improvement and create learning opportunities that will have the greatest impact on student learning.

References

American Association of State Colleges and Universities. (2006). Teacher induction programs: Trends and opportunities. *Policy Matters, 3*(10).

Aronson, E. (2000). *Nobody left to hate.* New York: W. H. Freeman.

Barker, R., and Gump, P. (1964). *Big schools, small schools: High school size and student behavior.* Wake County, NC: Issues Committee of Wake Education Partnership.

Bennett, R. E., Persky, H., Weiss, A. R., and Jenkins, F. (2007). *Problem solving in technology-rich environments: A report from the NAEP technology-based assessment project,* No. NCES 2007–466. U.S. Department of Education, National Center for Education Statistics. Washington, DC: Government Printing Office.

Billing, S. (2010). Five rules separate high-quality service learning from community service. *Principal Leadership, 10*(6), 26–31.

Birman, B., LeFloch, K. C., Klekotka, A., Ludwig, M., Taylor, J., Walters, K., Wayne, A., and Yoon, K. S. (2007). *State and local implementation of the No Child Left Behind Act, Vol. II—Teacher quality under NCLB: Interim report.* Washington, DC: U.S. Department of Education, Office of Planning, Evaluation and Policy Development, Policy and Program Studies Service.

Bloom, B. S. (1985). *Developing talent in young people.* New York: Ballantine Books.

Bond, L., Jaeger, R. M., and Hattie, J. A. (2000). *Accomplished teaching: A validation of national board certification.* Washington, DC: National Board for Professional Teaching Standards.

Bonner, L., Klahre, J., and Chavez, L. (2009, June 24). Bullying bill passes in tight vote. *Charlotte Observer Online.*

Boudett, K. P., City, E. A., and Murnane, R. J. (2006) *Data wise.* Cambridge, MA: Harvard Education Press.

Bransford, J. D., Brown, A. L., and Cocking, R. R. (Eds). (1999). How people learn: Brain, mind, experience, and school. Washington, DC: National Academy Press.

Bransford, J. D., and Donovan, M. S. (2005). Scientific inquiry and how people learn. In M. S. Donovan and J. D. Bransford (Eds.), *How students learn history, mathematics, and science in the classroom* (pp. 397–420). Washington, DC: National Academies Press.

Bridgeland, J. M., Dilulio, J. J., Streeter, R. T., and Mason, J. R. (2008). *One dream, two realities: Perspectives of parents on America's high schools.* Washington, DC: Civic Enterprises.

British Broadcasting Company. (2007, January 30). Doubts over hi-tech white boards. *BBC News.* Retrieved from http://news.bbc.co.uk/2/hi/uk_news/education/6309691.stm

Bronson, P. (2007, February 11). How not to talk to your kids: The inverse power of praise. *New York Magazine.* Retrieved from http://nymag.com/news/features/27840/

Bruce, B. C. (2001). Constructing a once and future history of learning technologies. *Journal of Adolescent and Adult Literacy, 44*(8), 730–736.

Bryk, A. S., and Schneider, B. L. (2002). *Trust in schools: A core resource for improvement.* New York: Russell Sage Foundation.

Burke, J. (2009). Chemistry in motion. *Edutopia, 5*(1), 10.

Butler, K. (2008). Crafting strategic plans: Key principles to enhance k12 leadership. *The Free Library.* Retrieved from http://www.thefreelibrary.com/Crafting strategic plans: key principles to enhance K12 leadership.-a0176866945

Chea, T. (2009, August 11). California names first digital textbooks that meet standards for high school math, science. *The San Francisco Chronicle on the Web.* Retrieved from http://www.sfgate.com/cgi-bin/article.cgi?f=/n/a/2009/08/11/state/n111611D86.DTL

Chrispeels, J. H., and Martin, K. J. (2002). Four school leadership teams define their roles within organizational and political structures to improve student learning. *School Effectiveness and School Improvement, 13*(3), 327–365.

Christensen, C., Horn, M., and Johnson, C. (2008). *Disrupting class: How disruptive innovation will change the way the world learns.* New York: McGraw-Hill.

Christensen, S. L. (2004). The family-school partnership: An opportunity to promote the learning competence of all students. *School Psychology Review, 33*(1), 83–104.

Coates, J. M., and Herbert, J. (2008). Endogenous steroids and financial risk taking on a London trading floor. *Proceedings of the National Academy of Science USA, 105*(16), 6167–6172.

Coleman, J. S. (1990). Foundations of social theory. Cambridge, MA: Harvard University Press.

Collaborative Communications Group and Edna McConnell Clark Foundation (Producers). (2002). Looking at teacher work: standards in practice [Video]. Retrieved from http://www.middleweb.com/index.html

Collins, J. (2001). Good to great: Why some companies make the leap . . . and others don't. New York: Harper Business.

Columbia Accident Investigation Board. (2003). Columbia Accident Investigation Board Report, (Vol. 1). Retrieved from http://caib.nasa.gov

Council for Exceptional Children. (2005). Universal design for learning. Upper Saddle River, NJ: Prentice Hall.

Council of Urban Boards of Education. (2005). 2005 annual school climate survey. Alexandria, VA: National School Boards Association.

Council of Urban Boards of Education. (2008). What we think: Parental perceptions of urban school climate. Alexandria, VA: National School Boards Association.

Coutu, D. (2009). Why teams don't work. Harvard Business Review, 87(5), 98–105.

Covey, S. R. (1990). The 7 habits of highly effective people. Tampa, FL: Free Press.

Coyl, D. (2009). Kids really are different these days. Phi Delta Kappan, 90(6), 404–407.

Cuban, L. (2001). Oversold and underused: Computers in the classroom. Cambridge, MA: Harvard University Press.

Cushman, K. (1996). Looking collaboratively at student work: An essential toolkit. Horace, 13(2), 5–17.

Daniels, S. R., Arnett, D. K., Eckel, R. H., et al. (2005). Overweight children and adolescents: Pathophysiology, consequences, prevention and treatment. Circulation, 111(15), 1999–2012.

Daniels Fund. (2005). School-business partnerships: Seven strategies for success. Retrieved from http://www.danielsfund.org/seven strategies/Strategies/

Davis, M. (2009, March 26). Breaking away from tradition: E-learning opens new doors to raise achievement. Education Week, 28(26), 8–9.

Deal, T. E., and Peterson, K. D. (1999). Shaping school culture: The heart of leadership. San Francisco: Jossey-Bass.

de Brabandere, L. (2005). The forgotten half of change: Achieving greater creativity through changes in perception. New York: Kaplan.

Dede, C. (Ed.). (2006). Online professional development for teachers: Emerging models and methods. Cambridge, MA: Harvard Education Press.

Deming, W. E., and Walton, M. (1988). The Deming management method. New York: Perigee.

Dinkes, R., Kemp, J., and Baum, K. (2009). Indicators of School Crime and Safety: 2009 (NCES 2010–012/NCJ 228478). National Center for

Education Statistics, Institute of Education Sciences, U.S. Department of Education, and Bureau of Justice Statistics, Office of Justice Programs, U.S. Department of Justice. Washington, DC: Government Printing Office.

Donovan, M. S., and Bransford, J. D. (Eds). (2005). *How students learn: History, mathematics, and science in the classroom.* Washington, DC: National Academies Press.

Doubt over hi-tech white boards. (2007, January 30). *BBC News on the Web.* Retrieved from news.bbc.co.uk/2/hi/uk_news/education/6309691.stm

DuFour, R. (2004). Culture shift doesn't occur overnight—or without conflict. *Journal of Staff Development, 25*(4), 63–64.

DuFour, R., and Eaker, R. (1998). *Professional learning communities at work: Best practices for enhancing student achievement.* Bloomington, IN: Solution Tree.

Elias, M. J., Bryan, K., Patrikakou, E. N., and Weissberg, R. P. (2003). Challenges in creating effective home-school partnerships in adolescence: Promising paths for collaboration. *The School Community Journal, 13,* 133–154.

Epstein, J. L. (2001). *School, family and community partnerships: Preparing educators and improving schools.* Boulder, CO: Westview Press.

Farkas, S., Johnson, J., Duffett, A., Wilson, L., and Vine, J. (2002). A lot easier said than done: Parents talk about raising children in today's America. *Public Agenda.* Retrieved from http://www.publicagenda .org/press-releases/self-control-good-eating-habits-parents-new-survey-report-limited-success-teaching-their-kids-absolutely-essentia

Florida Department of Education. (2003). Florida STaR chart. *School technology and readiness: Planning and assessment guide.* Tallahassee, FL: Bureau of Educational Technology.

Foorman, B. R., and Torgesen, J. (2001). Critical elements of classroom and small group instruction promote reading success in all children. *Learning Disabilities: Research and Practice, 16*(4), 203–212.

Fuchs, D., Fuchs, L. S., and Burish, P. (2000). Peer-assisted learning strategies: An evidence-based practice to promote reading achievement. *Learning Disabilities Research and Practice, 15*(2), 85–91.

Fullan, M. (2008). *The six secrets of change.* San Francisco: Jossey-Bass.

Garnston, R., and Wellman, B. (1999). *The adaptive school.* Norwood, MA: Christopher-Gordon.

Goddard, R. D., Hoy, W. K., and Hoy, A. W. (2004). Collective efficacy beliefs: Theoretical developments, empirical evidence, and future directions. *Educational Researcher, 33*(3), 3–13.

Goleman, D. (2006). *Social intelligence: The new science of human relationships.* New York: Bantam Books.

Gordon, E. (2009). Five ways to improve tutoring programs. *Phi Delta Kappan, 90*(6), 440–445.

Greenwood, C. R., Carta, J. J., and Kamps, D. (1990). Teacher versus peer-mediated instruction. In H. Foot, M. Morgan, & R. Shute (Eds.), *Children helping children* (pp. 177–206). Chichester, England: John Wiley.

Gregory, A., and Ripski, M. B. (2008). Adolescent trust in teachers: Implications for behavior in the high school classroom. *School Psychology Review, 37*(3), 337–353.

Gregory, A., and Weinstein, R. S. (2008). A window on the discipline gap: Cooperation or defiance in the high school classroom. *Journal of School Psychology, 46*(6), 455–475.

Haager, D., Klingner, J., and Vaughn, S. (2007). *Evidence-based reading practices for response to intervention.* Baltimore, MD: Brookes Publishing.

Hackman, J. R. (2005). Rethinking team leadership or team leaders are not music directors. In D. M. Messick and R.M. Krammer (Eds.), *The psychology of leadership: New perspectives and research* (pp. 115–142). Mahwah, NJ: Lawrence Erlbaum.

Harrison, D. (2010, March 4). Technology turns students into educators in distance learning program. *T.H.E. Journal.* Retrieved from http://thejournal.com/articles/2010/03/04/technology-turns-students-into-educators-in-distance-learning-program.aspx

Hattie, J., and Timperley, H. (2007). The power of feedback. *Review of Educational Research, 77*(1), 81–112.

Hess, F. M., and Gift, T. (2009). School turnarounds: Resisting the hype, giving them hope. *AEI Education Outlook, 3*(2). Retrieved from http://www.aei.org/outlook/100011

Hirsch, Jr., E. D. (1988). *Cultural literacy: What every American needs to know.* London: Vintage Books.

Hord, S. (2008). Evolution of the professional learning community. *Journal of Staff Development, 29*(3), 10–13.

Individuals with Disabilities Act (IDEA). (2004). PL 108–446, 20 U.S.C. §§ 1400 et seq. Retrieved from http://idea.ed.gov/

Ingvarson, L., Meiers, M., and Beavis, A. (2005). Factors affecting the impact of professional development programs on teachers' knowledge, practice, student outcomes and efficacy. *Education Policy Analysis Archive, 13*(10), 1–26.

International Society for Technology in Education. (2007). *National educational technology standards and performance indicators for students.* Eugene, OR: Institute for Technology in Education.

iSixSigma. (2002, June 10). Determine the root cause: 5 whys. *iSixSigma.com.* Retrieved from http://www.isixsigma.com/library/content/c020610a.asp

Judd, C. H. (1908). The relation of special training to general intelligence. *Educational Review, 36*, 28–42.

Kennedy, M. (1998). *Form and substance in in-service teacher education. Research Monograph No. 13.* Madison: University of Wisconsin-Madison, National Center for Improving Science Education.

Kirst, M., Haertel, E., et al. (2006). *Similar students, different results: Why do some schools do better? A large-scale survey of California elementary schools serving low-income students.* Mountain View, CA: EdSource.

Kotter, J. P. (1996). *Leading change.* Watertown, MA: Harvard Business School Press.

Lee, P. J. (2005). Putting principles into practice: Understanding history. In M. S. Donovan and J. D. Bransford (Eds.), *How students learn history, mathematics, and science in the classroom* (pp. 31–78). Washington, DC: National Academies Press.

Levi, M., Torrance, E. P., and Pletts, G. O. (1955). *Sociometric studies of combat air crews in survival training.* New York: Beacon House.

Lin, X, and Lehman, J. D. (1999). Supporting learning of variable control in a computer-based biology environment: Effects of prompting college students to reflect on their own thinking. *Journal of Research in Science Teaching, 36*(7), 837–858.

Marsh, J. A, Pane, J. F, and Hamilton, L. S. (2006). *Making sense of data-driven decision making in education: Evidence from recent RAND research.* RAND Corporation. Retrieved from http://www.rand.org/pubs/occasional_papers/2006/RAND_OP170.pdf

Marzano, R. J. (2009). Teaching with interactive whiteboards. *Educational Leadership, 67*(3), 80–82.

Marzano, R. J., Pickering, D. J., and Pollock, J. E. (2001). *Classroom instruction that works.* Alexandria, VA: Association for Supervision and Curriculum Development.

Marzano, R. J., Waters, T., and McNulty, B. A. (2005). *School leadership that works: From research to results.* Alexandria, VA: Association for Supervision and Curriculum Development.

McLaughlin, M. (2000). *Community counts: How youth organizations matter for youth development.* Public Education Network. Retrieved from http://publiceducation.org/pdf/Publications/support_services/communitycounts.pdf

McLaughlin, M., and Talbert, J. (2006). *Building school-based teacher learning: Professional strategies to improve student achievement.* New York: Teachers College Press.

McQuade, F., and Champagne, D. W. (1995). *How to make a better school.* Needham Heights, MA: Allyn & Bacon.

Metiri Group. (2006). *Technology in schools: What the research says.* Cisco Systems. Retrieved from http://www.cisco.com/web/strategy/docs/education/TechnologyinSchoolsReport.pdf

Miller, R. T., Murnane, R. J., and Willett, J. B. (2007, August). *Do teacher absences impact student achievement? Longitudinal evidence from one urban school district.* National Bureau of Economic Research, Working Paper No. 13356.

Mischel, W., and Ayduk, O. (2004). Willpower in a cognitive-affective processing system: The dynamics of delay of gratification. In R. F. Baumeister and K. D. Vohs (Eds.), *Handbook of self-regulation: Research, theory, and applications* (pp. 99–129). New York: Guilford.

Mischel, W., Shoda, Y., and Rodriguez, M. L. (1989). Delay of gratification in children. *Science, 244*(4907), 933–938.

Mitroff, I., and Silvers, A. (2010). *Dirty rotten strategies.* Stanford, CA: Stanford University Press.

Moss, J. (2005). Pipes, tubes and beakers: New approaches to teaching rational numbers. In M. S. Donovan and J. D. Bransford (Eds.), *How students learn history, mathematics, and science in the classroom* (pp. 397–420). Washington, DC: National Academies Press.

Murphy, J. M., Wehler, C. A., Pagano, M. E., Little, M., Kleinman, R. E., and Jellinek, M. S. (1998). Relationship between hunger and psychosocial functioning in low-income American children. *Journal of the American Academy of Child and Adolescent Psychiatry, 37*(2), 163–170.

Nansel, T. R., Overpeck, M., Pilla, R. S., Ruan, W. J., Simons-Morton, B., and Scheidt, P. (2001). Bullying behaviors among U.S. youth: Prevalence and association with psychosocial adjustment. *Journal of the American Medical Association, 285*(16), 2094–2100.

National Center for Education Statistics. (2005). *Calories in, calories out: Food and exercise in public elementary schools.* Washington, DC: Government Printing Office.

National Center for Education Statistics. (2006). *Indicators of school crime and safety.* Washington, DC: Government Printing Office.

National Comprehensive Center for Teacher Quality and Public Agenda. (2007). *Lessons learned: New teachers talk about their jobs, challenges and long-range plans, Issue No.1: They're not little kids anymore: The special challenges of new teachers in high schools and middle schools.* Retrieved from http://www.publicagenda.org/files/pdf/lessons_learned_1.pdf

National Governors Association Center for Best Practices. (2002). *Mentoring and supporting new teachers.* Washington, DC: National Governors Association.

National Incidence Study of Child Abuse and Neglect (NIS-4). (2009). U.S. Department of Health and Human Services, Department of Justice, and National Center for Education Statistics. Retrieved from http:// www.acf.hhs.gov/programs/opre/abuse_neglect/natl_incid/ index.html

National School Climate Council. (2007). *The school climate challenge: Narrowing the gap between school climate research and school climate policy, practice guidelines and teacher education policy.* Retrieved from http://www.ecs.org/html/projectsPartners/nclc/docs/schoo-climate-challenge-web.pdf

Newmann, F. M., Smith, B., Allensworth, E., and Bryk, T. (2001). Instructional program coherence: What it is and why it should guide school improvement policy. *Educational Evaluation and Policy Analysis, 23*(4), 297–321.

Ocher, D., Bear, G., Sprague, J., and Doyle, W. (2010). How can we improve school discipline? *Educational Researcher, 39*(1), 48–58.

Olweus, D. (1993). *Bullying at school: What we know and what we can do.* Cambridge, MA: Blackwell.

Olweus, D., Limber, S., and Mihalic, S. F. (1999). Bullying prevention program: Blueprints for violence prevention, In D. S. Elliott (Ed.), *Blueprints for Violence Prevention Series* (Book 9). Boulder, CO: Center for the Study and Prevention of Violence, Institute of Behavioral Science, University of Colorado.

Ouichi, W. G. (1983). *Theory Z: How American businesses can meet the Japanese challenge.* New York: Avon Books.

Parker-Pope, T. (2009, February 24). The 3 R's? A fourth is crucial, too: Recess. *New York Times,* (Late Edition (East Coast)), D5. Retrieved from http://www.nytimes.com/2009/02/24/health/ 24well.html

Perkins, B. K. (2008). *What we think: Parental perceptions of urban school climate.* Alexandria, VA: National School Board Association.

Pfeffer, J., and Sutton, R. I. (2000). *The knowing-doing gap: How smart companies turn knowledge into action.* Watertown, MA: Harvard Business School Press.

Picciano, A., and Seaman, J. (2009). *K–12 online learning: A survey of U.S. school district administrators.* Needham, MA: Sloan Consortium.

Plank, S., Bradshaw, C., and Young, H. (2009). An application of "Broken-Windows" and related theories to the study of disorder, fear, and collective efficacy in schools. *American Journal of Education, 115*(2), 227–247.

Pomerantz, E. M., Moorman, E. A., and Litwack, S. D. (2007). The how, whom, and why of parents' involvement in children's academic lives: More is not always better. *Review of Educational Research, 77*(3), 373–410.

Public Agenda. (2002). *Half of parents say there is still work to be done when it comes to teaching their child to do their best in school* [Data file]. Retrieved from http://www.publicagenda.org/charts/half-parents-say-there-still-work-be-done-when-it-comes-teaching-their-child-do-their-best-school

Public Agenda. (2004). *Teaching interrupted: Do discipline policies in today's public schools foster the common good?* Retrieved from http://commongood.org/society-reading-cgpubs-polls-3.html

Public Agenda and Bill and Melinda Gates Foundation. (2010). *Can I get a little advice here? How an overstretched high school guidance system is undermining students' college aspirations.* Retrieved from http://www.publicagenda.org/reports/can-i-get-a-little-advice-here

Public Agenda and National Comprehensive Center for Teacher Quality (NCCTQ). (2007, December 12). *Teachers from alternative programs more critical of on-the-job support, lessons learned: New Teachers talk about their jobs, challenges and long-range plans, Issue No. 2* [Press Release]. Retrieved from http://www.publicagenda.org/press-releases/teachers-alternative-programs-more-critical-job-support

Reeves, D. (2008). *Reframing teacher leadership to improve your school.* Alexandria, VA: Association for Supervision and Curriculum Development.

Ritblatt, S. N., Beatty, J. R., Cronan, T. A., and Ochoa, A. M. (2002). Relationships among perceptions of parent involvement, time allocation, and demographic characteristics: Implication for policy formation. *Journal of Community Psychology, 30*(5), 519–549.

Sawchuk, S. (2009, March 26). Teacher training goes in virtual directions. *Education Week, 28*(26), 22–24.

Schwartz, D. L., Lin, X., Brophy, S., and Bransford, J. D. (1999). Toward the development of flexibly adaptive instructional designs. In C. M. Reingelut (Ed.), *Instructional Design Theories and Models* (Vol. 2, pp. 183–213). Hilllsdale, NJ: Erlbaum.

Schon, D. (1973). Organizational learning. In G. Morgan (Ed.), *Beyond Method.* Beverly Hills, CA: Sage.

Senge, P. M. (1990). *The fifth discipline: The art and practice of the learning organization.* New York: Doubleday.

Senge, P. M., McCabe, N. H. C., Lucas, T., Kleiner, A., Dutton, J., and Smith, B. (2000). *Schools that learn: A fifth discipline fieldbook for educators, parents, and everyone who cares about education.* New York: Broadway Business.

Sheldon, S. B. (2007). Improving student attendance with a school-wide approach to school, family, and community partnerships. *Journal of Educational Research, 102*(5), 267–275.

Shepard, L. A. (2001). The role of classroom assessment in teaching and learning. In V. Richardson, (Ed.), *Handbook of Research and Teaching*

(4th ed.), American Educational Research Association. Lebanon, IN: Macmillan.

Silva, P., and Mackin, R. A. (2002). *Standards of mind and heart: Creating the good high school.* New York: Teachers College Press.

Simpson, V., and Oliver, M. (2007). Electronic voting systems for lectures, then and now: A comparison of research and practice. *Australasian Journal of Educational Technology, 23*(2), 187–208.

Skiba, R., Michael, R. S., Nardo, A. C., and Peterson, R. (2002). The color of discipline: Sources of racial and gender disproportionality in school punishment. *Urban Review, 34*(4), 165–183.

Somekh, B. (2007). *Pedagogy and learning with ICT: Researching the art of innovation.* Florence, KY: Routledge.

South Dakota Department of Education. (1999). *Technology in teaching and learning: Training module.* Retrieved from http://th012.k12.sd.us/TRAINING SURVEY.htm

Stipek, D. J. (1996). Motivation and instruction. In D. C. Berliner and R. C. Calfee (Eds.), *Handbook of Educational Psychology* (pp. 35–113). New York: MacMillan Library Reference.

Swearer, S. M., Espelage, D. L., and Napolitano, S. A. (2009). *Bullying prevention and intervention: Realistic strategies for schools. The Guilford practical intervention in schools series.* New York: Guilford Press.

Surowiecki, J. (2004). *The wisdom of crowds.* New York: Doubleday.

Taylor, A. F., and Kuo, F. E. (2009). Children with attention deficits concentrate better after walk in the park. *Journal of Attention Deficit Disorders, 12*(5), 402–409.

Technology Counts. (2009). Breaking away from tradition: E-education expands opportunities for raising achievement. *Education Week, 28*(26).

Tomlinson, C. A. (2004). *How to differentiate instruction in mixed ability classrooms* (2nd ed.). Alexandria, VA: Association for Supervision and Curriculum Development.

Tuchman, B. W. (1965). Developmental sequence in small groups. *Psychological Bulletin, 63,* 384–399.

U.S. Department of Education, Office of Planning, Evaluation, and Policy Development. (2009). *Implementing data-informed decision making in schools—Teacher access, supports and use.* Washington, DC: Government Printing Office.

U.S. Department of Labor, and Bureau of Labor Statistics. (2008, March). Employment and unemployment in 2007. *Monthly Labor Review.* Washington, DC: Government Printing Office.

Wald, J., and Thurau, L. (2010, February 25). Taking school safety too far? The ill-defined role police play in schools. *Education Week, 29*(22), 24–26.

Walsh, W. N. (2000). The effects of school climate on school disorder. *The Annals of the American Academy of Political and Social Science, 567,* 88–107.

Waters, T., Marzano, R. J., and McNulty, B. A. (2003). *Balanced leadership: What thirty years of research tells us about the effect of leadership on student achievement.* Denver, CO: Mid-continent Research for Education and Learning.

Watson, J., Gemin, B., and Ryan, J. (2008, November) *Keeping pace with K–12 online learning.* Evergreen, CO: Evergreen Consulting Associates. Retrieved from http://www.kpk12.com/dowloads/KeepingPace_2008.pdf.

Wehlage, G., and Rutter, R. (1986). Dropping out: How much do schools contribute to the problem. *Teachers College Record, 87*(3), 374–392.

What Kids Can Do. (2004). *Students as allies in improving their schools—A report on work in progress.* Providence, RI: Author.

Wilson, J. Q., and Kelling, G. L. (1982). Broken windows. *Atlantic Monthly, 249*(3), 29–38.

Wormeli, R. (2010). Teaching in the middle: Honor roll? Really? *Middle Ground, 13*(3), 31–32.

Yoon, K. S., Duncan, T., Lee, S. W., Scarloss, B., and Shapley, K. L. (2007). *Reviewing the evidence on how teacher professional development affects student achievement.* (REL No. 033). U.S. Department of Education, Institute of Education Sciences, Issues and Answers Report. Washington, DC: Government Printing Office.

Index

CORWIN

A SAGE Company

The Corwin logo—a raven striding across an open book—represents the union of courage and learning. Corwin is committed to improving education for all learners by publishing books and other professional development resources for those serving the field of PreK–12 education. By providing practical, hands-on materials, Corwin continues to carry out the promise of its motto: **"Helping Educators Do Their Work Better."**